Be Tough or Be Gone

The Adventures of a Modern Day Cowboy

Tom Davis
as told to
Marilyn Ross

Northern Trails Press
P.O. Box 238
Lajarta, CO 81140

Library of Congress Cataloging in Publication Data
Davis, Tom, 1948–
    Be tough or be gone.
    Summary: A young man spends nearly six months taking a pack train from Texas to Alaska, experiencing many adventures along the way.
    1. West (U.S.)—Description and travel—1981– 2. Northwest, Canadian—Description and travel—1981– 3. Cowboys—West (U.S.) 4. Cowboys—Northwest, Canadian. 5. Packhorse camping—West (U.S.) 6. Packhorse camping—Northwest, Canadian. 7. Davis, Tom, 1948– . [1. West (U.S.)—Description and travel. 2. Northwest, Canadian—Description and travel. 3. Alaska—Description and travel. 4. Cowboys. 5. Packhorse camping. 6. Davis, Tom, 1948–] I. Ross, Marilyn, 1939– . II. Title.
F595.3.D39 1984   917.8'0433   84-6149
ISBN 0-914269-09-7 (pbk.)

Second Printing 2001
Printed in the United States of America

FINAL
DESTINATION

STARTING
POINT

Map of North America

Dedication

Dream for the Stars.
Reach for the moon.
For the sky is the limit.
The man without a dream,
Is a man without a future.

I dedicate this book first to the dreamers, because if I had not been dreaming about it, it would never have started. There were many who said that it couldn't be done.

Secondly, I dedicate this book to my grandmother and grandfather, Mr. and Mrs. Jim Fort, for their knowledge, backing, and support.

Third, to my father and mother, Mr. and Mrs. Al Davis, for their encouragement after the trip got started.

Fourth, but not least, to Sonny Chavez, for his believing in me and for the stock he helped provide at the start.

Last, and definitely not least, to the Elks Lodges, the Jaycees, and the Chambers of Commerce along the way who helped me out with feed, water, and support along the whole trip.

Tom Davis
La Jara, Colorado

Table of Contents

Part One

"Head 'Em Up, Move 'Um Out"

Everything started out wrong.

Just as the sun crept over the horizon, I led Mula out of the barn. She was a half-broke, raunchy mule, as big as she was ornery. Mula hadn't been used as a pack animal before, so I talked gentle to her to make her less scared. "That-a-girl, just take it easy ole gray mule. We're goin' to take quite a trip, you and I."

Either she didn't go for the idea—or she didn't believe my gentle talk—because the minute the load hit her back she came uncorked. Bucking and braying, she laid food, utensils and supplies every which way like a spilled box of matches.

It took almost an hour to gather things up and repack 'em in the pannier boxes that had been especially built to fit the length of her body. They were made of half-inch plywood, wrapped with metal bands to hold them together. Nylon rope straps hung them onto the pack saddle. The heck of it was I didn't know how to tie the stuff on and balance it out so it would be comfortable for her. Not only was the weight something new, but the noise spooked her as well. Hard as I tried, it seemed everything rattled and banged as I hoisted up the panniers. And so we went through several sessions of her dancing around, the saddle spinning and stuff scattering all over before she finally decided to settle down.

It wouldn't have been so bad if I could have endured all this fuss in private. But word of my crazy cross-country pack trip had snuck out. Relatives, well-wishers and news people with their TV cameras were gathering to see us off. Friends, good friends from my racetrack days who really believed I could do it, were there too. It was a hell of a crowd. I could feel a cold chill snake down my back when I realized a guy with a minicam had it pointed in my direction. Next thing I knew a reporter thrust a microphone in my face. Through my fear I heard myself saying, "When I hit Salt Lake City and drop down into the valley, I'll have green grass and clear sailin' from there on. Then it's north to Alaska!" All my 27 years had been spent around livestock rather than people. Never having been captured in the limelight before, I was scared stiff of being on TV. All I wanted to do was get away before I let everybody know I wasn't too sure of what the hell I was doing!

But before I could escape, the Exalted Ruler of the Elks called me aside. "Tom," he beamed, "The members of your Alamosa lodge asked me to give you this as a send off." He pressed a $100 bill into my hand.

The money would really come in handy because my pack train had just unexpectedly grown. The previous day I had been shooting the bull with a new acquaintance named Luke and he seemed very interested in my proposed six-month horse back ride. Luke was an everyday-looking guy with eyes as dark as teak wood. What I really noticed about him were his hands. They were huge by any man's standards and seemed never still. Just for the heck of it, I suggested, "Why don't you come along, Luke?" never thinking he would take me up on the idea. But next morning—January 29th, 1976—there he was, bedroll in hand, his Blue Heeler dog, Freckles, in tow. Of course, I had only provisioned for one person and had planned on having a spare horse. The spare, "Baldy," was coal black with white stockings and a bald face. He stood 15 hands high. Baldy became Luke's mount and Luke became my part-time riding partner.

I should have suspected at the beginning just how things would come down when Luke doubled up with laughter while I raced around after the raging mule.

Mula packed and ready to go (?)

With the farewells taken care of and Mula calmed down, it was time to get on with it. My horse was one I was familiar with from the racetrack. He was a nine-year-old bay thoroughbred that had proven a sound steed. I had named him "Thoroughbred." There was, however, one problem. He was accustomed to the flat type of saddle used at racetracks. Whenever I'd start him off with a western style saddle, he'd buck like wildfire. He didn't just crowhop; he really got it on!

And I knew he was going to now. I had my camera, canteen, shotgun and a slicker tied on the saddle. As soon as my butt hit the saddle he ducked his head and came unglued. People scattered, then made a rough semicircle to enjoy the impromptu rodeo.

There was no way I'd let him throw me! Off came the camera. Off came the canteen. Off came the shotgun. Off came the slicker. (One more jump and *I'd* probably have been off.) But by now he seemed worn out. I figured I'd gotten the buck out of him. Usually when you got back on him again right away, he would jump maybe once, then be fine. So I got everything tied back on, unhitched Mula from the post where she had been tied, got her lined out behind and climbed on Thoroughbred. He was as wild as before! Of course, this excited Mula.

She started bucking and loosened the pack saddle until it slid under her speckled belly. Once again pots, pans and bedroll scattered everywhere. I hung on to her lead rope, kept my seat on Thoroughbred and shouted "Whoa!". It didn't work. She wrenched loose and bucked across a field leaving a trail of stuff behind her.

It took five hours to catch Mula. During that time she tromped hard enough on my foot to break my little toe. A mongoose and a cobra would have been on better terms.

As our weary troop plodded out of El Paso, Freckles yelped happily and trotted alongside his master. Not so my dog. Edgar wouldn't follow. So a friend gathered up the dingo pup and handed him to me in the saddle. Thoroughbred wan't used to a dog on his back, so he started acting up again to show his displeasure.

Finally we were on our way. It was now early afternoon. The stock was tired. I was exhausted. "You know, Luke, after this morning, I wonder what the hell I'm doing . . . and why."

"You ain't the only one," Luke replied. "And judging by the wind, we're in for some mighty cool weather."

"Better make camp early today. We all need the rest. Besides, my damn foot feels like somebody's poundin' it with a sledgehammer! Think I'd better get this boot off soon."

About ten miles out of town we made camp on an embankment where the river was washed out. It was too steep for the stock to get down to water, so I had to lead them, one at a time, a half-mile down river where it flattened out and they could water. Just what my aching foot needed.

I wanted to hobble Mula so she could graze. Although she was used to a picket, she had never been hobbled before and she was not at all inclined to let me tie her two front feet together. She was as free with her kicks as she had been with her bucks. I fooled around about a half hour, then lost patience, put her on a picket line and found two stakes for anchors.

The flat, treeless land offered little in the way of scenic diversion. But it didn't matter; that would all change soon enough. Besides, I wanted to figure out how to work my new camera. I studied it awhile, played a few tunes on the harmonica and soaked my sore toe while Luke put together a meal of sourdough biscuits, beans and dried fruits my Mama had fixed for the trip.

We were tired and untalkative that night, both sorting out our feelings and why we were here. I thought about the cowboy I wanted to be and the cowboy I was. At 6 feet, 3 inches and 180 pounds I was long and lean. The girls seemed to like that . . . and what they called me was "sexy eyes." But I wanted to make my mark. To do something special—to really be somebody—to reach inside me and grab the best I had and give it to the world. Maybe this was the way. With these thoughts I crawled into my sleeping bag and was out.

I didn't sleep well. Some dogs down river kept barking and the coyotes were yelping, making the stock uneasy. My toe woke me throbbing from time to time.

We were up at daylight and breakfasted on sourdough biscuits, beans and coffee. I had brought salt pork, spam, honey, onions and Jalapeno peppers. I figured to eat a lot of onions and peppers so I wouldn't get colds. Getting sick could snuff out the whole trip faster than a shovelful of dirt puts out a campfire. I was prepared to stay especially well over the next six months. Although my face already felt chapped, growing a beard would soon help that.

The Mission Mountains outside of El Paso.

Amazingly, the stock lined up pretty well and we got under way without any problems. I had to admit my pack looked like it was put on with a spider web. Fortunately, Mula was becoming more accustomed to carrying a load.

I dozed a lot in the saddle that day. Edgar followed much better. But when he got thirsty and went to the river for a drink, he jumped a jack rabbit. Wouldn't you know the dern thing ran right under the thoroughbred's feet. It scared him and he lunged, grabbed the bit and took off. He headed straight for a cement bridge! In his panicked state, I couldn't stop him. There was a wide spot by the river edge, but instead of going there, the horse headed for UNDER the bridge! I had a choice: lay down over the saddle or bail off. I flattened against the saddle horn.

I was wearing a goose down coat. The yolk caught the underside of the cement bridge and peeled off like a banana skin. Feathers flew. Pulling off the coat, I rolled it up, hoping to save some of the down. Then I went back and gathered up Mula and

Luke and we got going again. "Old Thoroughbred doesn't have much gas left after that run," Luke observed with a devilish chuckle.

"Nope. But he's a good walker. Really strides out." I was using a flesh needle and thread from the vet supplies to sew together the dismantled coat. Little did I know I'd be using that same needle for much more serious work in the next few days.

The Thoroughbred Plays Hide... I Play Seek

"Let's go, Ed," I yelled at the lagging pup. Nothing. "Damn you, Edgar, I'm tired of messin' with you. I'm not gonna baby you. Be tough or be gone. I haven't got all day. We've got a flat six months to make this trip."

The dog sat in the dirt as we disappeared around a bend. "I guess he's not tough, so he's gonna be gone," I said. I felt sad.

After a few minutes Edgar appeared behind us. "By gum, he ain't either," Luke cried. "Here he comes around that damn turn. I thought we'd left him back there, didn't you, Tom? Looks like he done changed his mind."

"Guess he rested up a bit. Maybe he's a little tougher than we thought," I replied.

For sure the cold was tougher than I had thought it to be. I had on my long handles and my leggings, a duck-down vest, the down coat, a corduroy shirt . . . and I was still cold.

We made about 15 miles that second day. After pitching camp and eating dinner, we picketed the animals and watched as the mule walked against her picket rope, testing. She wanted the grass just out of reach, though there was plenty underfoot. Beyond was a sandhill crane out in the marshy water, his neck bent like a question mark. Here the mighty Rio Grande was only a foot deep, the water black in the deepening dusk. They had been through recently with a mowing machine and cropped the willows about two feet high. They looked like a row of sharpened stakes standing sentry. As I laid back and gazed into the fading sky, ducks and geese flew north. I wondered where they were heading and how far they'd get. I was beginning to realize this was a whole new way of life. Already the routine was grueling. I told myself that it was just getting used to it; that things would get easier as time went on. I hoped I was right.

Later that night I awoke to vicious growling and snarling. Low-slung bodies thrashed against each other a few feet away. It took me almost a full minute to grasp what was going on. Then I saw a pack of five dogs tearing at Edgar. They were fighting right at the foot of my sleeping bag!

I jumped up, grabbed my pistol and got off a couple of shots. The intruding dogs bolted. So did Thoroughbred. He broke loose from his picket and headed for the river. I figured he wouldn't go far. Besides, my immediate concern was for Edgar. Examination proved I had stopped the fight in time. He had a couple of bad spots, but was generally in okay shape. So we all settled down to try for more sleep.

The next morning I expected to find Thoroughbred huddled with the other horses. No such luck. So I grabbed a lead shank and took off to pick up his trail and track him. Each step was more agonizing as my broken toe shouted its protest.

I trailed him five miles before I found him standing by a fence across from some other horses. He had hit one of the cut willows on the river. His leg was laid open from the knee plumb up to his chest. The gash went down clear to bone and muscle.

I had pulled myself through the painful walk with the promise that as soon as I found the horse, I could ride him back. With a front leg like that, however, there was no way. I had on a new pair of boots, blisters on top of blisters, a very painful broken toe . . . and no choice but to walk back the five miles, leading the crippled horse. I walked. The blisters got worse. So did my attitude.

"Oh, my aching feet!"

When we got back to camp I drug out the vet supplies and tried to stitch up the five-inch cut. But I couldn't, so I pulled the flesh around it and taped it up. Then we started out for Las Cruces, New Mexico. It was a motley group: an injured horse, a dog stiff and sore from fighting and a leader who would have cheerfully cut off his own feet.

As we were trudging along here came a sheriff's car and pulled along side. "Wonder what the hell we did now?" I commented under my breath to Luke.

"Afternoon, gentlemen," the officer said. "Fellas from the Elks Lodge asked me to come out and tell you they're waiting for you. It's only about ten miles to Las Cruces. There's a packing plant just outside town where you can put up your stock."

"That's good news. Say, do you suppose you could get a vet to meet us there? My horse's got a nasty gash and needs doctorin'."

"Sure thing. I'll make all the arrangements. Well, have a nice ride in." The car made a U-turn and zoomed away.

"Think we can make it in two hours?" Luke inquired.

"I reckon. With people waitin' for us, we're sure gonna try!"

It was just after six o'clock when we rode into the yards at the packing plant. Nobody was in sight. "Wonder where that vet is?" I growled. "I want to get this horse taken care of so's we can get taken care of."

We unloaded the animals and sat around for about an hour. "Hell, I'm not waitin' for that damn vet all night. Let's snub Thoroughbred up to that post to make him stand still and then I'll stitch him up."

"You think we can do it ourselves, Tom?"

"Hell, yes. You hold up the off leg while I sew the other one." I got out a needle and thread and put six stitches in the horse's leg before he decided that was enough. The big brute reared up and jumped forward. I was pulling skin together and stitching with the flesh needle when he lunged forward. He stuck the needle plumb through my thumb, hit me in the mouth with his knee and knocked me sprawling.

I got up with blood dripping from my mouth. I could already feel my lips swelling. But that didn't bother me near as much as the needle stuck through my thumb! I yanked it out, cursed the damn horse, then bandaged him up. About that time, in saunters the vet.

"Fraid you're a little late. I already did what I wanted you to do," I informed him. But he still charged me $20 for the call, even though he didn't do a thing. I'd have argued more, but the Elk brothers were waiting and I was more than ready for the good meal I knew they had in store for us. We left Edgar at the packing plant and headed for the Elk's Lodge.

They gave us a steak dinner, drinks and put us up in a motel room. Boy, that hot shower really felt good!

Later that night an old friend, Sonny Chavez, got into town. Sonny is a short, stocky guy from Albuquerque—a horse trading, talking, drinking son of a gun. Times when I was broke, Sonny would always give me a few bucks to get me going again. He brought a pack saddle and horses with him. One was a little speckled Appaloosa that I immediately named "Appy." Appy was only 14 hands and about 700 pounds, but Luke decided he would make a good mount and switched to him. Sonny also brought a bay horse. But I'd been around racetracks enough to recognize that this horse was slightly crippled. He was lame up in the shoulder. "Don't think I'll keep him long, Sonny," I told my old friend as we headed in to have a drink.

Next morning when we went to leave I found that Edgar had taken up with the packing plant owner. The man fed him kidneys and Edgar—who came of cow dog heritage—helped work the alleyways and herd cattle. So we all decided the packing plant should be Edgar's new home, since he didn't really take to traveling much.

The terrain that day was rolling prairie with a little sagebrush and scrub brush. The sandy soil blew around. There were many fences with two strands of wire to step over. Part way through the day a German Shepherd pup started following us. He looked half starved. He followed all day and took up with Mula. Along the Rio Grande it looked like some good fishing holes, so we got out the poles to try our luck. Sure enough, there was a mess of catfish and carp for dinner that night. I fed the German Shepherd some and started calling him "Comealong." We stayed along the river for grazing and water; plus I purposely wanted to avoid the main roads to meet up with fewer people.

As we sat around the campfire that night Luke said, "You know people ain't got no idea how to estimate distance. People know how much time it takes to travel by car, but that's about it." We had passed some folks that day and asked how far it was to Hatch and they said not too far, about 16 miles. Then half a day later we met up with some more people and asked them the same question. They told us it was still 15 miles!

I limped over to stoke the fire and give Comealong a pat, when a young woman with a shy smile appeared in the ring of campfire light. It was a surprise to have company. She reminded me of a hippy the way she was dressed and with her long hair hanging down. She apparently could see I was footsore the way I walked.

"My house is over there," and she pointed to the north. "Looks like you could use some moccasins. I'll come by later and bring some soft leather." Luke offered her supper, but when she heard what we were having, she commented, "I'm a vegetarian. But I'll be back."

About an hour later, here she came with the promised goods. As she worked with the leather, we sat around and sipped coffee and shot the bull.

"These packs are interesting," she said. "I'm making a pack saddle if I can just get my mule broke. Every time I get close to him, he kicks me," she said, rubbing a spot on her leg. "He's a little gray mule, just a bit bigger than a Mexican burro."

That's the worst kind in the world to try and break," I said. "What do you do 'round here?" I stuck a branch on the fire.

"Just a little prospecting, that kind of stuff. I work at a rock shop and go out in my spare time. Well, here you go, these should be more comfortable for you."

"Oh, they feel great. A heap o' thanks!"

"No big thing. Good luck on your trip. I've got to be getting back," she replied, slipping away as quickly and quietly as she had come.

The horses were in a field of Johnson grass and they were really chomping on it.

"That old thoroughbred sure needs his feed," I said. "He's probably lost a good fifty pounds. Looks pretty wiry now. Probably take two weeks, his head stickin' in a hay manger, to put back on what he walked off these last few days." We would be feeding him grain soon and he'd have some good roughage along the road coming up.

"Gitting smart, the big bugger. He's tough to hobble. Won't put his feet together no more," Luke commented.

"That little leopard-lookin' horse's comin' along like a champ," I replied. "Don't know for the life of me why Sonny brought him to me, though. He knows I want big, stout horses for this trip. I like 'em from six to ten years old. A young horse is like a young person; they get tired and bored easy. A horse is in his prime at eight. And I really go for studs. They've got stayin' power for sure."

"Well, Appy may be little, but he drops his head and prances with real zip," said Luke. "Got a hell of a good rein on him, rides good, travels good, he's just small. Sometimes good things come in little packages."

"Time'll tell, time'll tell."

By four the stock was dragging and the dog's tongues were flags. We saw an old adobe church on the horizon with a lean-to that looked like it would serve well for the animals, so we headed there.

As we approached, a lady in blue denims, a madras shirt and hair pulled into a bun strolled out of the church with her hands in her hip pockets. "Hello," she called. "Where are you two headed?"

"Would you believe Alaska?" I called in return.

"Not hardly," she replied, shading her eyes from the afternoon sun.

"Well, that's the plumb truth. We're riding this here pack train clear to Fairbanks," I told her.

"If you're for real, you'd better come in and get some supper under your belt with such ambitious plans," she invited. "My name's Pat and this is Ray," she said, motioning to a large man who had come up next to her.

After Pat had filled our bellies with chili rellenos, she told us what they were doing there. "We're restoring this old church. I'm a wood carver and he's an artist. I make my carvings from the pictures we found here in the church. We even rebuilt the steeple with adobe blocks we made ourselves."

Restored church at Hatch, New Mexico.

"But how do you live? I mean, what do you do to keep yourselves?" Luke asked.

"We barter," she explained. "We've got a big chili garden for trading purposes and sometimes we use our horses to help people and they give us stuff in return." They had two palominos that were stabled in the lean-to with our stock.

"This place is really fascinating. The last padre who occupied the church was a wino. He stole everything. Stripped the church bare and hawked it all to buy hooch. You know what else?" she continued. "They used to bury the priests under the floor of the church when they died."

"What the hell for?" Luke inquired.

"They believed it would keep their religious powers in the church."

"Whew! What a weird idea!" Luke commented.

Interior of old church with wood carved statue of a padre.

Pat went on to tell us Hatch was settled in 1880 and that the Indians used to keep the settlers run out of the area. The settlers would flee to the hills. They were so afraid of the Apaches they would go without water rather than show themselves. Sometimes they even died of thirst.

We stayed in Hatch an extra day, watching Pat and Ray work and enjoying her tales of the church and surrounding area. She sent us off on the next leg of our journey with a breakfast of sourdough hotcakes, eggs and green chili. Some feed!

How
It All Began

We were riding down a country lane headed for Array, New Mexico. I was riding Baldy to give the Thoroughbred a rest. The cold had eased up some and it was a peaceful ride. We passed lots of orchards.

"Trees look like feather dusters, don't they?" I commented to Luke. "Big business in this part of the country is raisin' pecans." I had no more gotten the last word out of my mouth than Baldy spooked and started rearing.

"What the Hell? You stupid sonamugun! You've seen a cow before. Ride this thing a 100 miles and then he spooks from a damn cow!" I said pulling tight on the reins and shouting, "Whoa!" After a couple more jumps, Baldy decided the cow wasn't really a threat after all and settled down.

"Boy, you don't know with that one. Got downright upset there. Sure like grain better'n cows," Luke laughed.

"Oh, they all go for the grain. They're still loosin' weight, though. Probably will 'til they harden up. Seem body sore. They're all movin' a little stiff. And I sure know how they feel. I can remember when I did my earlier ride from Tuscon, Arizona to El Paso. It was 312 miles and I did it in three days. Man was I sore! But I figured if I could do better than 100 miles a day over that road, the trip to Alaska would be a cinch. I felt on top of the world; like I could do anything!"

"How the hell did you happen to do this ride anyway, Tom?"

"One of the guys at the racetrack in Tuscon where I was workin' bet me I couldn't do it. Just after Thanksgiving in '75, I took him on. Decided to do it to commemorate the nation becomin' a Union in 1776. And it was also Colorado's 100th birthday. It's a personal way for me to celebrate the country and the states birthday."

"So you just up and did it?"

"Oh, no."

"I spent long hours in the saddle on bitter cold days to condition myself to the bad weather I would have to face. I talked to old-timers who taught me how to load a pack train and line out my horses in a string. They told me how to cope with the weather and how to ration my water. And I learned how to be my own vet, what supplies to take along, how to doctor saddle sores, what to feed the horses and mules to keep 'em sturdy."

"What did your family think of the idea?"

"Oh, most of 'em thought I was crazy. My folks said I wouldn't get as far as Albuquerque. They were afraid I'd get mugged. My biggest champion was my old Grandad, Jim Fort. He's in his 90's and was real sick when I sprung the idea on him. But he perked up right away and gave me all kinds of advice and good suggestions. He said I'd make it."

"Well, you've got to admit it is sort of a crazy idea, Tom. After all, nobody has ever traveled from El Paso to Fairbanks on horseback—in less than six months."

"Nobody yet. About the beginning of December I joined the Elks Lodge in Alamosa. I used the Elk's directories to send out form letters to the exalted rulers along the way to tell 'em I was coming. Bein' a pretty good card player, I figured I could pay for part of the trip with the money I won gamblin' in some of their private lodges."

"How did you know what stock and provisions to take? I mean, a pack horse can only carry maybe 200 pounds. It must have been a bitch to figure out what to take and what to leave behind."

"You better believe it! I figured I'd need four animals: one for campin' gear, one to carry feed, a saddle horse to ride and a spare. The saddle horse could handle a few more pounds because weight shifts. I picked up the thoroughbred from the track to ride. I got Baldy from Sonny Chavez. Only paid $250. Pretty good for a thoroughbred horse. Found ole Mula in Hooper, Colorado. Gave $400 for her. She was so dern big and lanky . . . about 900 pounds, over 15 hands and had a good stride. I called her "Mula" because an old Mexican sheep herder said she was a "Grande Mula" when he saw her being loaded. I could hardly catch her. Couldn't do much of anything with her at first; she was so wild. But then I like ratty stock. I believe as long as a horse or mule are fightin' you, they'll work for you."

"That's a fact. How did Edgar get in on the act? He don't seem like the kind of dog you'd have, Tom."

"Edgar was a last minute add on. I got a Blue Heeler pup when it was just 12 weeks old. Figured he could be both a watch dog and a companion. I really worked with that pup. He was so young I was afraid he'd get tired walkin', so I taught him to ride astride Mula. It was a funny sight to see him spread eagle on top of that mule's pack or behind the saddle on my horse!"

"Well, what happened? Why no Blue Heeler now?"

"Just before I was ready to leave, Dad accidentally ran over him and hurt him so bad I had to shoot him," I said in a flat voice. "That's when I got Edgar. He was almost a year old. I named him after the man I got him from. Sure turned out to be hard-headed didn't he?"

"Yes," agreed Luke. "Kind o' like his master."

"I'm gonna ignore that comment. You wouldn't believe the list of stuff I had to get in my pack. Besides a change of clothes there was a slicker, cold weather gear, my camera and tape recorder, a 12-gauge shot gun, a .38 pistol, ammunition and my hunting knife. Not to mention my fishing pole and tackle, a gallon canteen, Coleman one-burner stove, fry pan, coffee cup, silverware. Let's see, what else? Oh, yeah, a veterinarian first aid kit too. What's good for the animals is good for me. And I had a set of horseshoes per animal, a rasp, nippers, nails. Wow, what a lot of stuff!"

"All I can say is you must of planned on being mighty hungry."

"Hungry? Oh, I see. You know damn well I packed feed for the animals and grub for myself. I had honey and beans and flour and peanut butter. Oh, and my Mama fixed me a bunch of dried fruit to take and I loaded up on hot peppers and onions to ward off colds. It's a wonder I didn't need five pack animals!"

"Harvey Hostletter hauled me and my stock to El Paso. After I sold two studs to Sonny in Albuquerque for $600, paid Harvey and bought all those dad gum supplies, all that was left was $75 to make the trip on. When the Elks gave me that $100, I stashed it away for emergencies." Little did I know then how many "emergencies"—both financial and otherwise—there would be before this trip ended.

Tale From
An Old-Timer

Joe and Marie Griffith were old hunting friends of my dad's. They had a place near Array about a mile off the road out in the mesquite beside the Rio Grande. There was just enough brush cleaned off around the house for Joe to keep his junk stored. And did he ever have a bunch of junk! He purposely kept it that way so he could trap and shoot fox, skunks and bobcats. Trapping and shooting are Joe's major pastimes . . . that and raising bees.

We scattered a bunch of chickens going in. Joe kept them around to attract the predators. The chicken eggs they didn't gather and eat were left for the skunk, bobcat, fox and weasel to eat and to rot where they lay around the acreage. You could step on a rotten egg almost anywhere.

We put the animals out in their corral about a quarter mile from the house. They had running water and electricity at the corral—but carried water for the house. They figured it was easier to carry it for themselves than for the livestock. Pretty good logic at that.

"See that big old vat out there by the shed?" I asked Luke. "That's where he melts the honey out of the comb. That big old open pot sits there and he builds a wood fire around the bottom of it, like they've done for a hundred years. None of that gas heating for Joe. His honey is real good. Richest stuff I ever ate."

Joe sauntered out to greet us in his usual unhurried way. He wore an old pair of jeans hitched up with suspenders, a denim shirt and untied shoes. Joe rarely tied his shoes. Just slowed him up puttin' 'em on, he said. All he's ever done is hunt and fish and raise bees. Never worked at a regular job for long. As usual, his false teeth peeked out of a shirt pocket. He hardly ever put them in, even when he was eating.

Joe & Marie Griffith give us a warm welcome.

"Good to see ya, boy!" came his hearty welcome. "You're a sight fer sore eyes. Come on in and say howdy to Marie." Marie, short and dumpy, was puttering at the stove. She's a cook to end all. I knew we'd eat dern good at the Griffiths. "Here's my boy," she exclaimed proudly pouring everybody coffee. Joe's brother, Ted, sat down with us. He was tall and skinny; the typical old cowboy with tattered clothes, shirttail out and hat cocked back.

Joe and Marie built their house all by themselves. It was one of those "three rooms and a path" houses. The walls were decorated with coyote and bobcat hides, deer skins and racks of horns. The room was littered with stuff, but homey. Joe's two coon hounds were curled up in one corner. Comealong and Freckles did a tail-wag-sniff-get-acquainted-dance, then laid down and went to sleep. We got to talking about calling animals.

"We've tried callin' deer and coyotes, both," I said. "I never have been able to call 'em in. Talked to guys that swear up and down they can call 'em in."

Joe started telling us things, his arms waving up and down. I had heard his stories often enough that I knew some of them by heart.

"There's a lot of difference in callers. You learn to call, you can make a wrong note that's no good. This one guy and his son they called in and killed 19 coyotes in two days over at Ortiz awhile back. Forty-two teams went out. Guy and his son killed 115 altogether.

"My brother-in-law was trappin' and one of the game wardens asked him why he didn't get out and call to the trap. Well, he couldn't call. Warden said he'd come down and call up some, and he did. Called up three of them. So my brother-in-law decided he'd go out and try it. Got up early. Wife said, "What you doin'?" "I'm goin' out and see if I can call up a coyote or two!" So he took his rifle and shotgun, said if he didn't get a coyote, he'd do some bird hunting.

"He went down there and set against the bank. Couldn't get any coyotes in close enough to that shotgun. Sat there and worked and worked. They'd fool around out there, he'd call a little, and they'd get a little closer, but just out of range. Settin' there with his back against a bank, he heard something directly behind him. He looked around and they's two right there. He grabbed his shotgun and killed both of them."

As the story ended Ted was rolling a cigarette. He seemed to spend fifty percent of his time rolling a cigarette and the other fifty percent trying to keep it lit. Believe he smoked more matches than cigarettes. I was eating some of Marie's homemade biscuits with honey and Luke was sipping coffee.

"Bobcat is the hardest thing for you to get to see," said Luke. "If you haven't got everythin' just right, he'll crawl up there to you and you'll never get to see him."

"Best luck I ever had was callin' 'em where I could see 'em," said Ted as the ash fell off his roll-yer-own. "If you get on a ledge where the wind's right, they got to come over that ledge, you c'n be all right. But you c'n lose em, cause, like I say, they'll be from here to the door and you'll never see 'em."

When Old Joe got to talking it was hard to believe he was in his seventies. He was all energy. "That brother-in-law of mine was calling coyotes in. Sonofaguns will just slow up and listen. And you'll call and here they'll come. He's had 'em just run right in, practically fall right on top of him. And, dang, he throws his call down and grabs his gun, and they slunk away. He can tell they was there 'cause the stench is there.

"If a fella goes out in a pair, he don't have to move. He wants to stay put and he don't have to move his hands or nothing. Let the partner do the calling or the shooting and you can be ready for them. The moving is what gets you in bad. If you ever move, they spot you. If they's three of you, you pert'-near got to get down, let one guy do the calling. One of you gets where you can look one way, one the other way. Then you don't have to move to look 'round."

Ted jumped in: "There's one old boy was out callin' one night and two bobcats crawled onto him. I tell you that's where the fightin' starts."

"You bet," I said. "Fight'd be on for sure then."

Marie poured me another cup. She seemed real glad to have a kitchen full of chattering men. Old Joe got to talking about wolf hunting. I'd heard some of the story before, but he had a lively way of telling it that kept you interested.

"Now I had one over on the Pecos. I had on a pair of bullhide chaps, was on horseback and he was running about three hundred yards ahead. He got in this arroyo, 'bout six feet wide and as high as this ceiling. He just run up and hit that and laid down. Well, I couldn't do nothin' on my horse, so I stepped off and was gonna get that rope on him. When I hooked him around the flank, he turned on me. Grabbed my leg there with them bullhide chaps on. He wouldn't turn loose. You could tell he had holt of you all right. I just reached down and pulled out my wire pliers and banged him over the head. I caught five that morning."

"I like chasin' them" I said. We talked about how wolves

32

would stiffen up after they'd been run several miles, especially if they stopped or ran through cold water. Old Joe knew about running wolves.

"Some of them are pretty smart. We'd been over there at Salt Creek, three of us, wolf hunting. Got pretty tired and it was about two o'clock. So we laid down in the shade and took a little snooze. Awful tired. Got into Salt Creek going back and spied a big ole wolf. 'Spread out here and we'll get him,' I said. I'm riding a pretty good horse, so I tole everybody I'd take the north side. 'If he comes down it I'll chase him up there for you guys. Put that lobo down next to the creek so we can push him toward the water.'

"That old wolf seen what he was into, but I pushed my horse to head him off. I pushed this old filly off that hump to get down next to the water to get a run at him, and he spotted me. When he did, he just stopped. He knew he had done sold out. He crossed across that water. He laid off about fifty-sixty yards. Then it hit him. He just set down. There he set."

"Hit that cold water, he's hot, it's all over," I said.

"You know, he couldn't even get out of that setting position. Kid went out in the water, dropped a rope on him and picked him up like a toy doll. He was in sad shape. Died in just a few minutes. They can't take that running. We run him eight or nine miles, and it just pushed him too hard. When he hit that cold water it was too much fer his heart . . ."

"Just like a pony," I put in. "You get out there on the race track and run a pony a hard race and then don't cool him off, he'll sure get stiff and sore. Coyote, if he ever stops after a hard run, just let him set there a little bit and he's yours. He's all right as long as he keeps travelin' and a-lopin' along."

"I used to do LOTS of dang trappin' and huntin' down there around Roswell," said Joe. "Used to trap for them ranchers down there, for bounty. Then I got to working for salary bounty. Had about 125 traps. Usually didin't get 'em all out on them ledges 'cause they had something else for me to do around there. Them days they only paid $30 a month salary, and they'd give you $5 bounty. I could make more money there in a week's time trapping than I could working for salary."

We got to talking about stray dogs. Trouble, pure trouble.

"People haul 'em out of Cruces and El Paso, bring 'em up here and just throw 'em out," explained Marie. "They don't want 'em. Well, poor dog's gotta eat. He'll come around here and first thing you know he's killin' somebody's chickens or he's killin' pigs or sheep. They get to runnin' in packs."

"That's where we had trouble with our sheep," I said, remembering the fourteen mutilated carcasses I'd found in the spring. "The dang dogs come out of town. Now I can clean out four or five coyotes botherin' the sheep, and don't take me very long to do it. But you get a pack of them darn dogs comin' out of town and killin' 'em, and you gotta work after it to get 'em. They're smart and hard to hunt.

"I had a well house once. Went out real early in the afternoon, crawled inside that well house and set out there all night. Like to froze my tail off. The temperature was about zero. I set there and waited like that for three or four nights waitin' for 'em to come back. I knew they'd be back, but I didn't know just what night they was goin' to hit. They won't come back every night, you know."

Marie said, "And there's another pack back in just a few nights; tell 'em 'bout the trouble we had, Joe."

"We was gone about two hours and a half and got back here and it was gitting between sundown and dark. They was chickens all on top of the house and anywhere you look on anything high was chickens. I knew something was wrong. I hurried in and got my shotgun and headed off out to the chicken pen. I met one dog still at work. I knocked him down. There was 32 chickens layin' out there. They never eat a chicken. They just come in and go to killing. Well, if they do you that way, they can wipe you out pretty quick when they just keep coming back."

About that time, Marie got in a stew with one of their hounds. She was nosing around where she shouldn't have been. "That mangy dang dog. She's into everything!"

Pretty soon, old Joe got to talking about deer hunting. He told about a guy who had shot a deer and was fixing to carry it back to camp 'cross country. "I knew he was going to get into trouble, but I didn't say nothing. He had that old deer on his shoulder, weighed about 125 or 130 pounds. He was really huffing and puffing. Got to a cliff and he was thirsty enough to go right off into the river and get him a drink. Well, by God, it was 30 or 40 feet straight off. So, like a darn fool, he took off his gun and pitched it out there in the sand of the river bed. And he pitched the darn deer off, too! I watched him from on a hill, seen what he done. Then he had to go back about a quarter of a mile to get around to the bottom and come back to where his deer was.

"By damned, I went up and jumped another little bunch of deer and I followed them quite a ways. Never did get no dang shot.

"So I come back to help him. When I got off the bluff and got around, he'd gone out in the creek with that damned deer and he was just leading him up the stream in that water."

Joe laughed his free and easy laugh. The rest of us joined in.

"I said, 'What the hell 're you doin'?'" recalled Joe. "He said, 'Hell, it's a whole lot easier to float him along in the water.' 'Yeah,' I says, 'but he won't be worth a damn eatin'!"

"Spoil him, sure as hell," I added, still laughing. There was more to the story.

"His damned old meat will be as mealy as all get out. I said, 'You can't eat that sonofabuck. You just as well throw him in the ditch now and leave.' 'No,' he said, 'I'm takin' this thing in.' I said, 'All right. Damned, you'll find out what I'm tellin' you.' Got him on into camp and strung him up. I says, 'If it's me, I'd pull that hide off that damn thing right now and dry him out as much as I could, if I was figgering on eating him.' 'Hell, no,' he says. Next morning I walked out to his darn deer and I says, 'Hey, you'd better go home and take that thing in.' 'Oh, hell, he'll keep another day.' Next mornin' he got up and he said, 'By God, that sonamugun *is* gettin' a tainted smell.'

I said, "Yeah, I'll bet by the time you get him home and start cuttin' him up, he'll be dog's feed." Sure enough, that's what it was when he got home. He said, "I'll never do THAT again." Joe told him, "You'll learn."

Settlin' Down
To Travelin'

After a two-day stay, lots of stories and Marie's good vittles, we were fixing to leave.

"Them pack boxes ought to be higher," Joe instructed nudging the panniers a bit. "Easier on the mule." He should know. Joe packed many a mile with mules and he's covered more territory than I ever will. "Here, let me give ya a hand and we'll get 'em on sound."

We left Joe's place heading for Truth or Consequences, New Mexico. By that afternoon Comealong's feet were sore as heck. They seemed to hurt so bad he didn't know which one to limp on . . . had to walk on three feet all the time. He was crossing the road so slowly at one point that a car had to stop and wait for him.

He learned when we stopped, to take advantage of the break. He'd promptly lay down and rest or lick his paws. Luke started callin' him Old Flop Ear, because he had a broken ear that hung down. "Gives him character," I declared. "Hell, it might even stand up before this trip is over. He's really turned into a good partner."

"He sure set up a fuss back there when you climbed into Joe's truck and he thought you was gonna leave him."

"I'll say. Never heard such howlin' and whinin'. Like a

damned coyote, yelpin' and wantin' to go with us."

"He's gonna be a big one, that's for sure. Must be close to 60 pounds now. If he grows up to fill out those bones, watch out."

That night when we made camp I felt sorry for him so I cut the tongue out of my hiking boots and spent all evening making boots for the dog. The stock was chewing on their omaline, happy as hogs in a potato patch. "These horses just now gettin' the habit of—when we stop—goin' ahead and grazing and takin' care of themselves. Mules are smarter than horses. Mula doesn't fool around. We stop—she eats. Horses finally got themselves wore down to where they walk instead of trying to run all the time."

"You notice how sore, the bay is?" Luke asked. "Not a very good doer. Taking lots of feed."

"Yep. Course hasn't helped that we haven't been able to trade saddles yet. He must have lost a hundred pounds, mostly his winter fat. Baldy's different. Grabs a few bites here and a few bites there. Doesn't look like he's lost any weight. Looks solid standin' there."

"Noticed the little Appy fell back today for the first time," said Luke. "Looks body sore, the way he moves."

"Get to Albuquerque, Sunny'll take him back and give us another one," I replied.

The next morning Luke made coffee and warmed up the left over dinner stew while I lengthened the pickets so the stock could do some morning grazing and hung out our bedrolls to air. We decided to also make pancakes for breakfast, then carry the extra ones as bread for lunch.

Then we broke camp. All the gear got packed back into the pack boxes and panniers; then I balanced the load the way Joe showed me. I put the booties I'd made on Comealong's tender feet, saddled up and started off. That is, all but Comealong started off. He stayed behind and dutifully chewed off all four boots, then hobbled along on three legs to catch up.

"You happen to hear him last night?" I asked.

"Not me. I slept like a hibernating bear," replied Luke.

"Crazy dog gets up and prowls around. Real quiet like, mind you. Last night he never left our campsite. But I woke up twice and he was patrollin' our territory, makin' sure everything was okay. When he's asleep, got to have his nose right under my head. Thinks he should use my pillow, I guess. We're gonna have to get it straight, Comealong, that it's *MY* pillow. Some dog!"

Lake near Truth or Consequences, New Mexico.

More terrain outside of "T or C."

The rolling plains were now intersperced with gullies etched like wrinkles on the face of an old man. Foothills rose around us. The sky was blue and clear with a bright sun overhead.

"Think it's about time we head for the freeway. Loosin' too many miles by followin' the river. Goin' with its winding path, we travel 10 or 12 miles, but actually only cover about six. Hate to leave this peace and quiet."

"You and me both."

About six miles further on we reached the main thoroughfare, but there was a cattle guard across the road, making it impassable for the animals. "Let's go down that embankment and around the guard," Luke suggested. Going down the steep dirt bank the pack slipped on Mula, spinning to her belly and scattering things every which way. She panicked, broke loose and even got the thoroughbred to bucking. "Hell, here we go again!" I shouted, trying to settle down the horse. With that, Mula jerked the lead loose and galloped back down the road with the pack dangling from her belly.

She went straight for this lady's garden, which was all rowed up and ready to plant. What with me chasing Mula around, we proceeded to completely total the poor lady's garden. She came out of the trailer house laughing her tail off and helped me catch Mula. Fortunately, she was as playful as a colt herself and didn't much mind our rodeoin' in her garden.

"I'm real sorry, Ma'am." I told her with a big grin. "Let me pay you somethin' for the damage we did to your garden."

"No, cowboy, that's all right. I've been watching you from the time you dropped down off the road. The entertainment was worth it!"

About five miles further, the border patrol stopped to jaw with us. Truckers honked at us as they went by. The first time one of those big rigs pulled his air horn, I thought Mula was going to leap out of her skin. Of course, we had another spill before I finally soothed her with a lot of gentle talk. She was one spooky mule—even afraid of bicycles!

I had a CB radio, but couldn't get on the 19 crystal, which is what the truckers use. My little job had no antenna and was just a three-channel outfit. But there was Bill Mack, who was quite a truckers DJ. He was with a Fort Worth-Dallas radio station and put out the word to the truckers to wave or stop and see if I needed help when they passed.

I led our pack train down the middle of the freeway. It was all controlled access where you can't get on or off except at especially constructed places. Along the way some Easterners stopped to ask what ranch we worked on and where it was. They thought we must of been on our way to town for supplies. After all, why would anyone ride smack down the center of the road in the middle of nowhere with a bunch of livestock in tow?

By this time our clear skies had clouded over, a strong breeze was blowing and rain threatened. Midafternoon it started spitting on us. "Let's stop and put our slickers on," I shouted at Luke. We went another 200 yards and I'll be darned if we weren't plumb out of it. I was really hot inside the slicker. And Thoroughbred was going crazy with the flapping of the dern thing as the wind whipped it against his flanks. We were only to glad it was a brief shower and to be shed of our rain gear.

I often fished along the Rio Grande after we'd made camp.

41

That evening we found a half-way decent campsite and unsaddled the horses. After we tied Thoroughbred, Baldy and Appy to a sturdy tree, we unloaded and unsaddled Mula. By now we had a regular routine established. One of us would get feed out of the boxes and fill the grain sacks and nose bags and hang them on the animals, while the other would make a fire and put the grain boxes around it for seats. Then we'd line out our groceries and cook supper. After eating, I would usually water the stock, then spread them out on picket for two or three hours of grazing. Then we'd lay out our bedrolls and sit around the campfire drinking coffee and talking or making notes about the day. Some nights I broke out my harmonica. Before turning in I'd shorten the picket lines for protection against cutting or tangling.

Riding along the next day the traffic had thinned some, so I broke out my harmonica and started to play a tune. The minute the sound reached her ears, Mula started braying. Maybe she though it was so bad, that was her way of protesting. I went through old western songs like "Destiny," "Skyriders" and "Streets of Lorado." Then I played a tune called "Big Flying You" about a cowboy riding a brama bull. Luke gave me a sideways glance every once in a while, but I'd just ignore him and keep on playing.

Things were pretty routine that day and we made camp in the bottom of an arroyo on an old ranch with a windmill. The windmill must have been the only water for some distance as there were tracks from bobcats and coyotes all around the area. After we got things set up, I went back up the arroyo to hunt for rabbits for supper. There was an old barn off to one side, so I decided to investigate. It turned out to be a lucky find. Inside was a lot of stored hay. Looked like it had been around for quite some time. Well, I figured the rancher wouldn't mind my feeding my animals and it saved me spending seven bucks a bale for hay. The horses and mule were down right grateful.

As it turned out, it was good they had a big feed that night. We didn't know it then, but they were in for some very treacherous traveling.

Not a Drop
To Drink

All the next day we kept a look-out for water. But even though we pushed far north, there was still no sign of it. Finally, after about 25 miles we spied a construction site. Snooping around, we found they had a well for running sprinklers. The stock drank thirstily. It had been a long ride. There was nothing for grazing, as they had cleared the area and hadn't planted any grass yet. But I was grateful for the water. We were carrying grain, so the animals didn't go hungry.

I started calling Comealong "Woof" sometimes, 'cause he would sit at the campsite and if he heard a noise he would give a gentle, "woof." Seemed like he didn't want to spend the energy to really bark full out. That night he kept prowling around and woofing a lot. Every time I got up I couldn't see anything. Must of been game of some kind stalking us. Woof just gave his little bark and sometimes Freckles chimed in. But I knew he wouldn't let anything into our campsite. A while back a couple of dogs had ventured too close and Woof was up and ran them off in no time.

Next morning we headed off in the direction of San Antonio, New Mexico. "It's a far piece," Luke commented, looking at our battered map.

"Yup. Probably take two good days to get there," I answered.

But we hadn't counted on how dry it is in that section of the country. As it turned out, the animals had no water that night. We had barely enough to see us through.

"Only thing I can do is slow down the pace," I told Luke in an edgy voice as we started out the following day. "We're goin' to drop down to ten, maybe 15 miles a day. Poor suckers won't be bothered as much by thirst if we don't push 'em." The weather was cold, about 30 degrees with a lot of wind and some rain. The cold made traveling easier. Colder it was, the less the lack of water affected the stock. Even so, the horses noses were mighty low to the ground by the time we spotted a house with a well the next day. They had been almost three days without water!

I'd driven this stretch of road a hundred times, but had never realized what beautiful scenery it was. When you travel so goldang fast, you don't pay attention. Now I was seeing it foot by foot. And I was really experiencing it. There's a sense of progress when you ride over a hill and anticipate what you'll see over the next rise. Looking out across the desert and hills there were miles and miles of brilliant wildflowers. It was like nature had spread out a huge carpet of color. And the fragrance! The air was perfumed with a wonderful sweet smell from all the blossoms. Made me feel really alive and part of it, like the animals. We also started seeing a lot of cottontails and three kinds of quail. There were blue quail, topknots and some partridge.

We pulled into San Antonio late in the afternoon. "You know, Luke, I've been cravin' a hamburger for about a week. Let's see what we can find."

After picketing the stock we went downtown and treated ourselves to a couple of hamburgers and a couple of beers. Then we nosed around downtown. That took all of five minutes. There was a bar, a cafe, a post office and a gas station.

A little further ahead we noticed a junkyard. "What a place to spend the night," I exclaimed. "It's off the freeway so we won't be bothered by the public."

"Yeh. A great place to hide," agreed Luke. "And look, they got a hose over there so we'll have plenty of water." That settled, we proceeded to make camp amid smashed cars, scrap iron and miscellaneous pieces of junk.

From there we moved up through Socorro. "Grocery store ahead," I called.

"Let's get some candy bars and stuff to break the monotony," came Luke's reply.

"Okay. I want to get a soda pop anyway."

A radio was blaring as we entered the little market. "Take advantage of General Electric's Happy Birthday America celebration. It's going on right now," an announcer crooned. I thought about how I was celebrating America's birthday in my own special way. It sent a shiver of excitement down my spine. When I next heard the radio a weather forecaster said that Ogden, Utah had just gotten four inches of snow. "No sweat there. We're three weeks away. It'll be clear sailing by then," I told Luke as we each gathered up a few more groceries, paid our bill and headed out.

After spending 75¢ for a can of pop, I knew I was in trouble. My original idea had been to live off the land and graze the horses. It was now obvious that wouldn't be totally practical. My 75 dollars wouldn't last long at this rate! I never really stopped to think about how much a trip like this would cost. Just figured I wasn't broke, 'cause I had the 75 bucks. Now I realized how little that money would buy. "Man, I sure hope we can find an Elk's Lodge that's got a game goin'," I told Luke. "I've always had pretty good luck with poker and with the dice. That should fatten the kitty some."

"What the hells that there 'neath the bridge?" Luke asked, pointing down about 15 feet.

"I'll be damned. Old Joe told me there were jaguars in this neck o' the woods. Looks like three of 'em. Somebody must of skinned 'em out. Two adults and a kitten I reckon." The kitten was hardly bigger than a chihuahua dog. The others resembled

45

greyhounds. Whoever killed them skinned the heads out to the tails, excepting the paws. They had cat feet that looked speckled from where we were.

"Suppose somebody killed the whole family and skinned 'em out, then threw 'em in the creek. Figured the rain'd wash 'em down into the lake and nobody'd be the wiser."

Later that afternoon we noticed the skys were almost as full of traffic as a California freeway. "Them whooping Cranes?" Luke asked. "No. Sandhill Cranes," I replied. "There's a game refuge near here. It's like a layover spot on their migration route. Good grass around here too."

We had kicked off freeway 25 earlier in the day and were on an old road headed into Belen. All of a sudden we came on the dangest sight. There framed in a doorway stood a young women clad only in a bathrobe. She waved briefly, then scurried inside. In a couple of minutes she was back out in boots, shirt and levis.

"Can we water our horses?"

"Sure," she replied, eyeing the bandages on Thoroughbred's leg. "Can I get some medicine for him?"

"We have everythin'. But sure appreciate it. We're goin' out there a ways, stop, clean up and camp."

"Well, we got a barn and corral right here you can use. Got hay and everything you need."

So we camped by the barn door after kicking the horses into the corral and carrying water for them. We fed all the hay we wanted for nothing. The lady told us she was from New Jersey.

Then she ducked in the house and returned with an armful of brand new towels, vaseline, bactine, peroxide and washcloths. She worked on the thoroughbred like she was a natural vet, taking off the bandage, cleaning his wound and re-dressing his leg. It was a blessing she doctored Thoroughbred because—unbeknownst to us then—we would soon have to prove he was not being mistreated.

46

Love Those
Belen Beauties!

Riding along a few miles south of Belen we happened across two young ladies who waved us down excitedly.

"Hi, I'm Myrt and this is Cindy" said a vivacious brunette. "We been listening all about you on the radio. Are you really headed for Alaska?"

"You bet. All the way to Fairbanks," I replied.

"Well, I want your picture . . . and how 'bout an autograph?" came tumbling from the girl's mouth.

"Gosh, I don't know about the autograph," I said hedging. I'd been telling people I couldn't read or write to get out of doing so much autographing. Guess it was about time to break down, though. So we dismounted, signed their autograph books and inquired the way to the local Elks Lodge.

A few blocks from the Lodge, Bert and Cindy McKinley—more admirers—stopped to chat. They also insisted on photographs. In the process of picture taking, however, their Polaroid broke.

"Shows your ugly mug stops the camera," chortled Luke.

The McKinleys directed us to a laundromat where we could do some much-needed clothes washing, then we headed for the Elks where newspaper reporters were waiting to take pictures and do a story.

The Belen Elks were down right hospitable. They put us up in a hotel and made us welcome at their club. When we asked about Myrt and Cindy, we were told they were a couple of nuts . . . real fun girls. After a few drinks, we headed out of town three miles to stable the stock with an old friend, named Herman Coffee. He was a horse trader and salesman I'd known a long time. After visiting with Herman a couple of hours, we were hauled back to Belen and the McKinleys' came by to take us out for dinner and dancing. Once again Myrt and her friend came into the picture.

Out on old highway 85 heading towards Albuquerque the next day, it was raw and cold. The wind whipped at us and rain pelted down. A gray scum of cloud hung overhead. Looked like it might snow anytime. We went through the Isleta Indian Reservation. Both there and on the other side, people kept wanting to talk with us. The word had definitely gotten out! Kids were flipping the peace sign and one hippie ran out and shouted "Hey, that's beautiful, man beautiful!"

The SPCA, having also heard about the trip, stopped us to make sure we were treating the stock alright. They made us unpack all the animals to check for saddle sores or other problems. That was just what was needed to put us behind schedule by several hours. The guy in charge eyed Thoroughbred's leg something fierce, but when he inspected it, he couldn't find anything to complain about. (Boy, was I thanking the lady who had fixed him up!) The only real thorn in anyone's side was the humane society in mine! As it turned out, this was to be the first of many hassles with them.

Further along the highway as we were riding by some railroad tracks, a newspaper photographer appeared. He ran along in front of us for about three-fourths of a mile furiously taking pictures.

After we made camp that night, I laid back and looked up into the heavens. There was a pattern in the stars I had never seen before. Looked almost like a Mexican sombrero. "Ever tried to figure out the star patterns . . . especially Virgo and Taurus?"

"Not me," replied Luke. "The only stars I want to see are in some gal's eyes."

"That's a fact. But I mean I've laid hours tryin' to find a bull or a scorpion. Danged if I can see it. Milky Way, now that's across there. That's somethin' I can find. That and the Big and Little Dipper."

Sure smelled good. A little crisp. A little moist; like rain in the air. It kind of cut through the dryness and helped hold down the dustiness.

About nine o'clock here came the Belen beauties, Myrt and Cindy, again. They were all gussied up. "What say you fellas come down to the Sidewinder with us? We'll have a couple of drinks and do a little dancing," they coaxed. It didn't take much urging to have us raring to go. In fact, after we got tired of the Sidewinder, we went to the Quarterhorse Lounge for more of the same. Think the girls wanted to say they'd been out with the guys riding to Alaska.

The next morning we were big news in Albuquerque. "Would you believe we got the top of the front page in the *Albuquerque Journal*!" exclaimed Luke. And who had the front page of the other local paper? None other than Patricia Hearst.

"We're doin' pretty good when two small time cowboys can compete with someone as big as a Hearst," I replied.

Sonny Chavez and his brother, Marshall, plus two or three others from the Elks Lodgs were waiting for our arrival at the stockyards. I was to pick up another horse and do some more trading with Sonny. It was no question but that Thoroughbred, with his buggered-up leg, had to be replaced. I also decided to trade off Baldy since he was smaller than I liked for the long haul. In return I got a bay horse I named "Apple Jack" and a four-year-old bay gelding as a loan horse.

I had been ridding a Bon Allen saddle from the beginning of the trip. It was a big roping saddle made especially for me— heavy leather, cottonwood and rawhide covered trees, plus extra

49

padding on the seat. It was real comfortable. I never came up sore from riding it. Gave almost $500 when I had it custom made a long time ago. But it was entirely too heavy for my purposes now. I traded it with the agreement that when the trip was over I'd be able to return and trade back for my saddle or buy back the Bon Allen from the man who took it.

That first night in Albuquerque we spent at the fairgrounds. But the second night a friend, who was the general manager of the Airport Marina, arranged for accommodations there. When I got checked in, I called Myrt and invited her to visit. After all, she had wheels and I was afoot. Not much fun in a big town. She came up and we had a hell of a party. But I suspected, with a tightening stomach, that this luck might not hold.

The
Unplanned
Pow Wow

During the course of the following day we passed several groups of Indians who would stop and say hi and offer us a beer. Being one to enjoy a cold one, occasionally I accepted. That was my big mistake.

Myrt looks me up to pay a visit.

After we made camp that night, Myrt visited with her little girl, Katrina, who was celebrating her 3rd birthday. The child was shy as a newborn fawn. We were chatting around the fire, when here came a handful of Indians weaving crazily and clutching a couple of six packs. They gathered up more firewood and soon had flames shooting 20 feet up into the air! Then they started whooping and hollering and did a sort of war dance.

"What the hell's goin' on here?" I shouted. "You're gonna catch those trees on fire!" But the Indians seemed oblivious to anything I said. By the time they had wound down a bit, here came another group with a case of beer in tow.

"Good God, you'd think we were in the middle of their reservation," said Myrt with a worried expression on her face. She pulled Katrina over closer to her. Just then a patrol car squeeled up and two uniformed Indian policemen came running over. At the sound of brakes, all the Indians who could walk headed for cover behind trees and bushes. Within 30 seconds only a handful—too drunk to have any real idea of what was happening—remained. They were carted off by the police.

But as soon as the patrol car left, here came everybody padding out of their cover to cavort once more around the fire or gather in huddles of two or three and look at us menacingly.

My knife was laying on the pack right next to me so I could watch it. Given a chance, I had few doubts that one of them would take it. I really didn't want any trouble as we were greatly outnumbered. My hope was that they would run out of beer, get bored and leave. Fat chance! Well, I had certainly learned one thing: whenever an Indian offered me a beer in the future, I would suddenly become a teetotaler!

The roaring fire seemed to serve as a signal shouting "party here!" Within an hour we had a new bunch of Indians and a fresh supply of beer. The patrol car arrived again and carted off a few more who didn't manage to slink into the underbrush. But the party grew back to full force almost as soon as they left. There was absolutely no way to get rid of them! I finally decided they meant no real harm. They had simply adopted our campsite as the place to party for that night. It certainly left little room for sleep or restfulness, so I started telling Myrt and Katrina about the trip.

"Can't carry a sidearm into Canada."

"You can't do what?" Myrt inquired.

"Can't go into Canada with a pistol. They check it at the border and seal it in a plastic bag, then they give it back to you. Course it better be sealed when you come back out. Figure I'll just stick mine down in the grain, carry it right on."

"I'd let 'em seal it," said Myrt. "That way if you ever get in a bind you got it handy to use."

"Oh, you can carry your rifle," I said. "They just don't want you to have handguns."

"Looks like these here Indians don't want you to have any knife, either," she said gesturing to where I had put down my knife.

"I'll be damned! They must of swiped it when we were talkin' about Canada," I retorted angrily. "Nice folks."

"Can't win 'em all, I guess. Just hope they don't get any smart ideas about using it!"

I caught a glint of fear in Myrt's eyes as the flames danced from the fire. Figured if I could get her mind off the Indians, she wouldn't be so nervous. "See that mule over there?" I asked her pointing to where Mula was chomping hay. "I remember when I broke her to the rope. Took me three nights and four days to catch her, she was so danged wild. Wore out five horses doin' it. Poor thing had been chased by motorcycles, so she was really spooked. But I knew if I caught her she'd be worth the fight. It was quite a thing to rope her, out there with a thousand acres for her to run in. Guy owned her told me 'I'll let you have her for $300—if you c'n catch her.' It sure was a challenge!"

"How'd you finally get her?" asked Myrt, warming to the story.

"Built a trap around a water hole. I'd chase her, then back off and let her into the water. When she got used to the idea, I sprang the trap. Then I had to teach her to lead. Tied a lead rope on her and the other end to the back of a pickup. Then I drove slow about four miles down the road. That broke her to lead real fast."

Finally at 4:30 the Indians had wound down and were willing to go on home—after they decided I was serious about NOT making them breakfast. Seemed like we had barely gotten to sleep when here came a half dozen of them. My watch showed seven o'clock, my disposition showed wear. But when I saw they had hay for the stock and a 55 gallon drum of water for the horses, I had to chuckle a little. Luke and I had decided we weren't even fixing breakfast for ourselves that day. Anything to get rid of them and get on the road! After saying goodbye to Myrt and Katrina, we loaded the stock and headed out.

The day started out pretty good. Cold, but nice. By afternoon we were in the middle of snow and wind. It got colder and colder. I swung down off the highway. About a quarter of a mile away there were some old corrals that were made out of willows laced together. Just then it started hailing. Not just little peas of hail, big chunks almost the size of a cue ball! By the time I got down to the corrals and got all the stock in, I was soaked clear to my skin and so was everything else. I was already mad at the mule for acting so balky. Being wet and cold made me all the madder. "Hell, what a storm. Even our bedrolls are wet clean through!" I shouted at Luke in disgust. I looked around for some dry firewood to start a fire. It was hard to find anything that hadn't gotten soaked, especially with hail stones pelting down my back.

About now the trip didn't seem like a very good idea. I was real discouraged. I remembered my slogan of Be Tough or Be Gone and wondered if I was really tough enought to make it.

While I was feeling sorry for myself, Luke was trying to rustle up a cup of coffee. He finally got a cup poured. Boiling hot it was, in a tin cup. It was still bubbling when he set the cup down on a pack box.

Turning to holler at me, he slipped in the mud and sat plumb down on that boiling coffee. As it spilled on the seat of his pants he let out a banshee wail and leaped to his feet. His arms flew around like propellers to keep him from falling in the muck. The muck he missed, a stump he didn't. Luke fell face first. Boy, did I laugh at the sight of him trying to miss mud and going in the other direction. Really wasn't so funny though. When I helped him up, he had several cuts on his forehead and blood dripped from his chin. I hurried to dig out the vet first aid kit to clean him up a bit.

"Don't you go gettin' near me with no needle," he screamed.

"No fear, buddy. I'm just gonna wash off those cuts a bit," I assured him.

It was a miserable night. Everything was wet. We couldn't get the bedrolls dried out, so we lay shivering in their damp embrace. It was snowing like mad and the wind was howling. I never spent any colder night in my life! About three o'clock we got up and tried to coax a fire into existence, but the wet wood wouldn't cooperate. So we got the dogs and went and crawled down in a wash to help break the wind. We curled up with the dogs to wait out the sunrise. When a weak sun crept over the horizon, we got up and broke camp. I was never so glad to be up and on our way!

We stopped and brewed some coffee and made a quick breakfast when the wind and snow slacked off a bit. Then we hit the trail again. I wanted to make as much time as possible, hoping that we could outrun the storm. That didn't happen. But we got lucky in another way.

Along the road folks had told us about a couple named Texas Slim Lassiter and his wife, Barbara. Slim was said to have invented a new car engine. When they saw our bedraggled pack train coming along the road, they came out and invited us to stop and rest a bit. Slim was poppin' proud of his new fireplace. We were only too happy to share its welcome warmth!

"Hope you don't mind us comin' through your cattle guard," I said wrapping my cold, stiff fingers around a cup of hot coffee.

"Oh, hell, no. Weather like this, only makes sense to help a body," replied Slim in a booming voice that matched his huge bulk. "Don't get many folks in this here ghost town anyway. You

o feel free to spend the night. Been hearin' lots 'bout you on
e radio."

Texas Slim and his family lived at La Catina. He had
ivented an engine (he pronounced it "Injun") that was self-
istaining. It took a 12-volt battery to turn over the generator to
et the thing started. After that it would create enough juice to
:eep the alternator going, thus keeping the battery charged to
zenerate enough power in the alternator to operate the engine.

"Got the dang thing patented," he told us. "Course you'll
never hear no more about it. Sold the patent to an oil company.
They can't let an engine like that hit the market. Don't cost
nothin' to operate it. I got one in my old Cadillac. That baby
cruises at 60 miles per hour," he told us proudly.

The thought of going down the road in a plush, comfortable
car at 60 mph was very inviting. It made me even less anxious to
go out into the bitter cold for the next leg of our journey.

Ice 'n Sleet
'n Frozen Feet

To keep our minds off the chill the next day, Luke and I talked a lot about horses.

"I'm sold on pine tar, honey, snuff and turpentine," commented Luke. "They're great for doctoring horse cuts."

"Gal back in Belen told me she liked aloe vera plants. Said to cut them in half and lay 'em right on the cut. Claimed she had a rash from sand fleas in Florida and within a few minutes of puttin' on the aloe vera, the itchin' was gone," I said.

"I'll be danged. Suppose she's right?"

"Don't know. Think that's the same stuff they use in womens face creams and for ulcers and stuff, though. Must be good stuff."

"You ever notice how white-footed horses got soft feet?" Luke inquired.

"Sure. An' black-footed ones got hard feet. Don't know why nature made 'em that way, but it's a fact. Albino's goldang usually got bad eyes too. An' most paints. We used to call those paints moon eyes."

We were swapping stories about favorite horses when all of a sudden a covey of police cars flew by us, then pulled off the road about 300 yards ahead.

"Holy shit! What we done wrong now?" exclaimed Luke.

"Beats me. Whatever it is, they sure came in force. Half a dozen cars up there!" The cops piled out and came walking back to meet our string.

"Howdy, boys," the first said with a friendly wave. "We been readin' all about your ride to Alaska and we want to get some pictures and hear more about it."

With a sigh of relief, Luke and I began reciting the story. It was beginning to wear as thin from re-telling as an old saddle blanket does from use.

When we got just beyond Cuba, New Mexico, we met a man who had a little boy named Billy. They had a spread about five miles northwest of town and invited us to spend the night at their ranch. By the time we got there, it was snowing again, so we were mighty grateful to have a place to put up. He led us to the bunkhouse and put our stock down in the barn, even turning his own animals out in the corral. Gave us hay and grain for the animals that night.

"Come on in and have dinner with the family," he invited. His wife put together a good meal of tacos and hot tamales. Afterwards we got to talking about hunting bear. I figured I was bound to get a grizzly up in Alaska. "Like to have me a big old grizzly rug," I said.

"Them grizzly get as big as the horses out there," put in our host. "That's a lot of bear."

"Takes a lot of ammunition to push him off," I said, telling about an article I had read on an Indian who killed a Kodiak with a snub-nosed .38. "The guy jumped out of a tree onto the bear's back and shot him behind the ear with a snub-nosed .38."

"Chances are he probably fell out of the tree and the dang gun went off," commented Luke. Everybody laughed.

When I woke the next morning there was four inches of snow on the ground. The morning was as cool as the backside of a pillow. Over a big breakfast of sourdough biscuits, eggs and pancakes, my new friend made me a present.

"Want you to have these here panniers, Tom. Bought 'em for myself to go hunting, but after looking at your old ones, you

58

need 'em a lot worse than I do." When I protested at his kindness, he insisted, saying, "Hell, I only go hunting once a year. You're gonna need these for a long time to come. It's settled."

People. They—and their good hearts—were becoming the highlight of this trip. Traveling in a car you pass thousands of people along the highway, 20 maybe 30 feet away. But there's no communication, no caring. When you travel by pack train you get a whole new perception of the goodness of people.

Treking across the Continental Divide.

We headed over the Continental Divide towards Counselor. Some folks stopped us on the road and suggested we lay over at the Trading Post. Man, it was a cold stretch. The snow was getting deeper and the road, no matter which way you wound around it, put you smack dab facing into the wind. We couldn't see 50 feet ahead of us. Everything was cold. Bleak. Bitter. My beard—at first just a bit of shrubbery—had grown to magnificent bushy proportions. It was caked with ice.

"Damn. It's so cold ridin' in the saddle. Let's get off and walk a bit. Maybe it will warm us up some," I said dismounting. The cold was so bad I couldn't tell when my feet hit the ground. I went to my knees. I didn't even know I had touched the ground. I got up and got the circulation worked back into my feet by walking a little bit. My fingers felt like frozen french fries. Face was chapped, ears numb. After I rubbed them some they felt prickly, like cactus spines were poking them.

Back in the saddle it was colder than ever. Nobody even got out of their cars to talk to us. They just drove on by. There were lots of truckers out that day. And you'd have thought you were in Texas instead of New Mexico. There was a raft of Texas license plates.

At Counselor we and the horses were put up in an old barn. There was no heat, of course, but the body heat of the animals helped to take some of the chill out of the air. I gingerly pulled off my boots and massaged and rubbed my feet. It wasn't until then that I realized I had frozen them. "And it don't look like things are improving none either," lamented Luke. Outside the snow was coming down and icicles hung from the corner of the roof like stalactites in a cave.

We made 18 miles the next day. It was a hard push all the way. Temperatures were below zero with wind and a little snow. I'd sit in the saddle as long as I could stand it, then get off and walk a ways. When I climbed down I noticed that ice hung off the stirrups. I froze my hands and ears that day. It was a long, desolate strip of road. No towns, nothing to break the miserable cold.

In the late afternoon we made camp at a little place called Nageezi. There was a deserted barn that Luke and I took shelter in. The stock we put in a corral just outside. The horses and mule were sore and needed to rest as bad as we did. I was really looking forward to having a couple of days off in Farmington . . . and to getting out of this blasted cold!

It was a long restless night. Woof barked a lot. Seems the Indians turn their horses loose all winter to fend for themselves. They kept coming close and bothering my stock. So I'd have to get up and chase them off.

Towards afternoon the next day the snow was more sketchy and the weather started warming up a bit. Probably because we were dropping down some in elevation. People began stopping us again—a sure sign that the bitter cold was over! They said we had lots of publicity in the papers and on radio and TV news.

It was a welcome dry camp that night. The snow and wind and rain had finally slacked off. But I still wasn't to get a good night's rest. About two o'clock there was a big ruckus. I woke to see Woof chasing a wild police dog out of camp. He went scooting like his fanny was being fanned by a blow torch. But the dang bugger tried to invade us two or three more times before the night was over.

I was weary in the saddle the next day and took a couple of catnaps. During one of them I became aware we weren't moving anymore. "What's goin' on?" I inquired with a start. "Mula won't go," replied Luke. "She came to a standstill and won't be bullied or coaxed no further."

"She's either sorin' up or her pack isn't balanced right. I'll have to find out why she quit on us." I knew it could be a burr or a wrinkle in the saddle blanket that was rubbing her. Or maybe the pack was uneven. If it wasn't balanced right, it would be uncomfortable and might make her refuse to budge. Sure enough, I found that the pack had slipped and the weight wasn't evenly distributed. She was communicating her displeasure in the only way she knew how. "Give me a hand, Luke, and let's get this thing adjusted. I'm in no mood to waste time out here. Farmington will be a lot more fun!"

A Hot Time
In the Old Town
of Farmington

We stabled the stock at the fairgrounds, then headed for the Elks Lodge. It was a nice dinner club overlooking the golf course. It was the first place where I was invited behind the scenes to gamble. Gambling was legal in a private club then. Back in their game room there's a crap table set up. That's my game; I love to shoot dice. When I go into a game, I have just so much allotted to lose. When that's gone, I quit. Or if I start winning with it, I'll take my original investment, stuff it in my pocket and go with my winnings. If I ever start down, then I may dish into the original investment, but no way will I go beyond. That night I came away with 75 bucks! Boy, did I feel good. I suddenly doubled all the money I had started with.

Later that night we went back to the Farmington fairgrounds where they were holding a dance. "Man, look at all those drunk Indians!" said Luke. Sure enough it was quite a sight . . . cars running into each other and everything. They must have wrecked 25 cars that night. No cops, either. They just drove off. Glad I didn't have a new car sitting in the parking lot. We checked the stock to make sure everything was alright, then bedded down for the night.

The next day my folks met us and we did some switching. I

sent back a bunch of stuff with them. After 400 miles, I'd weeded out what was unnecessary. They brought me a tent and some groceries and were interested to hear about the trip. Since I'd gotten this far, they extended their guess that I might make it to the Canadian border.

Sonny Chavez showed up that afternoon with a good looking paint mare. I decided to name her "Joanne" after Sonny's wife, a real fireball of a lady. The mare was an eight-year-old ex-rodeo horse that had never been broken to ride. Part of that afternoon we put on an amateur rodeo on the fairgrounds green as I battled to show her who was boss. Sonny took the bay gelding back with him. The other bay had a rope burn, so I doctored him and let all the stock rest that day. They all seemed to appreciate the break. Even the dogs feet were pretty well healed by now. Their pads had toughened so they could take the long walks each day. Today, however, they were content to frolic a little, then stretch lazily in the sun and nap.

On leaving, an Elk brother told me about a shortcut to trim 15 miles off the next stretch. Following his directions, I opened some gates and found myself on a Ute Indian Reservation. It was pretty riding. Plenty of grass and the stock was eating good. I began to train Joanne. Had to plow rein her at first. We stopped and put new shoes on Mula about mid-day, then resumed our progress. Luke and I made camp right in the middle of the reservation that night.

The next morning as we were packing up to leave, an Indian agent rode up. His attitude was as prickly as a porcupine. "What the hell are you doing here?" he shouted. Before I could answer he went on "You have absolutely no business on this reservation. You're trespassing. Where is the rest of your party?"

"What do you mean 'the rest of my party?' What you see is what we got."

"We received a report that there was a bunch of white men out here target practicing, busting bottles and raising cain."

"Well, I'm afraid your report is full of crap!" I retorted indignantly. "There's just the two of us and we haven't fired a shot."

"Maybe they exaggerate," he said more meekly. "But you're not supposed to be here. You're about half way across the reservation now, so there's no point in turning back. Just be sure and stay on the old dirt road and head on straight across."

I wasn't about to tell him, but he could have rested assured that we would stick to the road. We were in an area where gullies dropped 30 feet straight down. It sure wasn't a park where you went wandering any which-way over grassy knolls. We had definitely left the flatlands. Up ahead small mountains rose on each side of the road. But they were like a plateau on top, as if somebody had taken a saw and sliced off their peaks. The reddish layer of rock left on top almost looked blood-soaked.

Four-corners area by Colorado & New Mexico border.

Part way along that day we noticed some structures ahead. "What you suppose that is?" asked Luke.

"Dunno. Won't be a mystery long, though. We're headed in their direction." As we approached, there were several hogans in various stages of disrepair. They were made of timbers standing upright and laced together with rawhide. We weren't the only ones around, however. Two pickups were parked next to the largest hogan, which was nestled against a rock cliff.

Chief's hogan on Ute Mountain Indian Reservation
near Cortez, Colorado.

"Hello," called out a tall young man who ducked through the doorway. He was followed by three other young men and a woman. They certainly weren't Indians. I immediately thought of our run-in with the Indian agent and wondered if these people had felt his wrath too.

"Howdy," I replied. "Surprised to see you folks out here."

"Oh, we're archeologists. I'm Larry, this is Mark, Bob, Richard and Lindy." After we introduced ourselves they invited us in for a beer. They seemed anxious to talk.

"You're in the homeland of the Ute here. This area was abandoned about 1300 A.D.," Larry explained. "The hogan we're sitting in contains the skeletons of eight chiefs buried underneath."

"Wow! What for?" asked Luke.

"Well, they believed that the next-in-line should live here too in order to keep all the powers in the main hogan. See those drawings on the wall? They were put on with berry dye. That's why there's so much red." The paintings were of people and animals. One large buck deer predominated. "We estimate they're 100 years old," he continued with pride. "But tell us about yourselves. You must be pretty adventurous guys!"

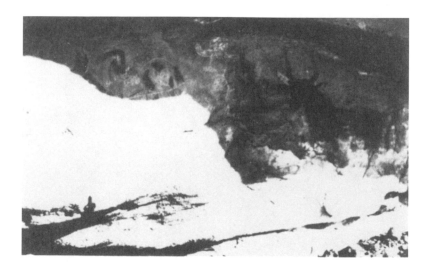

Ancient Indian drawing on cliff wall.

So once again I recited how the trip came about and what had happened to us so far. They were impressed. Being from back East, this was true cowboy stuff to them and they sopped it up like a sponge.

We ended up yakking most of the afternoon, so I decided to make camp there that night. Only problem was a lack of water. The solution came when our hosts volunteered to take one of their pickups and go into Cortez. They got some buckets and stopped at an Indian village and hauled water for my stock in two five-gallon buckets.

By morning the weather had turned cold again. We had a combination of rain, snow and wind. "Boy, I can't wait 'til we get to Salt Lake and green grass and clear sailin'," I commented to Luke as we headed out into the blizzard.

That night we made camp by the four corners area where the boundaries of Colorado, Utah, Arizona and New Mexico all come together. We had crossed over into Colorado and pitched our tent in the Mesa Verde National Park. It was 30 plus miles to Cortez . . . and the meanest mule I was ever to meet!

An Ornery Mule
Named Trashy

We woke early the next day and were saddled up and ready to go by daybreak. As the sun climbed over the horizon, the chopped-off mountains were bathed in an orange glow. It was as if all the cruel cold had been washed away and here was a gift of beauty and warmth. The sunrise reflected on the clouds and my spirits lifted with the fiery globe.

The Cortez stockyards served as "home" for the next two days. We rested up a bit and I got acquainted with an old saddle maker and had some tack repaired. It was time to search out some fresh stock. This seemed a likely place to do it. Met a fella by the name of Johnny and traded him the Bay for a sorrel gelding he called "Red." Appy was getting tired, so I traded him for a little brown mule. The mule had breeching marks and breast collar marks that showed it had been packed a lot, so I figured it was a good bet to help carry our load.

But when I got her to the stockyard and started to handle her, the dern thing just about tried to eat me! She bucked and stomped her foot and raised such a ruckus it soon became evident that she had never had a saddle on her back in her whole life! And here I was trying to handle her and get to know something about her . . . boy, was I learning fast!

The stockyard where we were staying was a mess. They had

held a sale the day before and there was 18 inches of mud and manure all down the alleyways. Absolutely slushy. So what does the mule do but spin around and take off down the alleyway with me hanging onto the rope and trying to take eight-foot strides to catch-up! Finally, I couldn't keep up, so I let go of the rope and fell flat on my face in all the gunk. That's how "Trashy" got her name. I called her Trashy because she was just trashy to handle. When I finally caught her and got her settled down enough to really look her over, the damn breeching marks proved to be just the width of a clipper blade!

I was sleeping on the floor inside of the sale ring, as were some other cow pokes. Met a guy who had bought a beef there the day before at the sale. He was butchering it out back. I went out and helped him and he gave me the flanks and some other scraps. There was seven or eight pounds of beef in all. I cut it into strips and, using the fat from about the gut for grease, fried it on my coleman stove. Then I rolled it in chili pique. It's like cayenne pepper, only hotter and is a great preservative. Presto. I had beef jerky. It was perfect because I like hot foods and chili pique wards off colds. I put it into plastic sacks and stuck it in my saddlebag.

Cortez was a mighty friendly town. The Elks had a big lodge that sits out on the golf course and has a country-club atmosphere. Everybody was bringing their daughters in to meet me, so I really got wined and dined. They also took a lot of pictures and passed the hat. Hat passing was getting to be a regular thing when we went in places where they had heard about us. Was getting so I could count on ten or fifteen bucks in donations. The Elks and Chambers of Commerce would also give me film for the trip. That helped too. The Cortez Elks Lodge sported a crap table. With me and the dice old buddies, I got in the back room and came out 50 dollars ahead.

Out of Cortez the road followed near a creek that was lined with willows. It was pretty scenery and the day was clear and crisp. We made it to a point just outside of a tiny place called Pleasantview when an elderly lady came out of her house carrying a jar of something.

"This is fer you, sonny," she said offering me the jar of

homemade raspberry jam. She must have been in her eighties. Said to put the stock in the corrals out back, come in, and have some supper. Turned out she was mighty lonely. Her husband had died and none of her kids or grandkids lived nearby. She had us put up camp for the night by the corrals and wanted to know what time I'd be leaving in the morning.

"Shortly after daybreak, Ma'am. Least I sure try to be on the road around sunup." Next morning when we awoke, the lights were already blazing in her house and the aroma of homemade biscuits and coffee left little to doubt. I fed the stock and we enjoyed her breakfast.

The next evening we made it into Dove Creek, a trek of barely under 20 miles. Just to be different, the weather was drizzly rain and miserable. A guy came out from the bar and invited us in for a drink. Well, one thing led to another, so we decided to put the stock up nearby at this guy's house, then go back and party in earnest.

When he realized I planned to leave him, Woof had a fit. Wanted to stay right in my hip pocket. I had to throw rocks at him or he would follow me everywhere. He flat didn't want to be left. Would whine and cry like a baby. Finally, he gave up and went and curled up by Mula.

Back at the bar things were in full swing. Luke spied a little chick he took a shine to and everybody came over to me to take pictures and get an autograph. They even pressed a few bucks into my hand.

Leaving the party later that night, I was going to walk across the field to get to the pens where the stock was. It was a plowed field that had turned into a muddy bog with the rain. I was unsteady as it was. With that—and the deep, clutching mud —it was just too much for my impaired balance. Over I went, rolling in the mud. By the time I reached the pens, I was a mess.

It wasn't until the next day that I realized just how much of a mess. The guy's two young daughters woke me up giggling and pointing. My face and beard were caked with dried mud, as were my hands. My clothes were plastered to my body and my sleeping bag looked like it had been wallowed in by pigs. The girls led me to the house where their understanding mother showed me to the shower and prepared a big, fancy breakfast. Unfortunately, there was little of it I, or her husband, could eat. Meantime, these kind folks had gathered up my down sleeping bag and had in it the wash machine. "I'll catch up with you and bring it out as soon as it's dry," he promised.

Sure enough, after I'd crossed the state line into Utah and was about half way to Monticello, here he came. I was feeling much better by then anyway. We had just found a 100 dollar bill laying in a ditch! We had found ones and fives along the road before, but nothing this big. Figured it must be a good omen. Boy, was I ever wrong!

About a half mile later Red managed to step on a nail and come up lame. When you're counting on your stock to carry either you or a load of supplies, it really hurts to have one out of commission.

By now I had put on enough miles that publicity was really rolling in. People were becoming aware of what I was doing and were enthusiastic. Just before Monticello, a newspaper reporter by the name of Miles Turnbull came out in the drizzle to meet me. He invited us to spend the night at his place and located a stable across the street for the horses and mules. He even called a vet to tend to Red. The fella came out, gave the horse a tetnus shot, then pulled the shoe and put a pad under it. He even donated his call and the shot. Quite different from the last experience I'd had with a vet!

The next day I led Red empty. We were traveling through the Utah canyon lands. Even from the saddle I could see skeletons of fish in the sandstone. They were all different sizes and shapes. Proves that all this area was once under water. We saw fossil prints too.

"Hey, look over there," I said to Luke pointing to the side. "That's Fat Lady Rock."

"I can sure see why," he replied gazing at the mass of rock that rose from the ground. It did indeed resemble a fat lady, with hips it would take *two* grass skirts to fit around! We were passing many interesting rock formations. If you let your imagination run wild you could make out animals and all sorts of odd things from their shapes.

"Fat Lady Rock" near Montecello, Utah.

A huge mysterious cave south of Moab.

"That was one hell of a cave we passed a mile or so back," Luke said. "Never seen one spread out like that. Kinda like somebody took a layer of red rock, left a space, then put another layer on top of it."

More of the canyon lands near Moab.

About half way to Looking Glass Rock we met up with a couple of gals who we got acquainted with back in Dove Creek. They followed us in their car and wanted pictures and personalized autographs for their kids. "You know, everybody talks about doing something like this, but nobody has guts enough to try it," one of them said. We talked for an hour or so, then they gave us some steaks they had brought out. We ate one and packed the rest. It was cold enough that nothing would spoil, 'cept maybe our dispositions.

Looking Glass Rock was our campsite that night. It is a beautiful natural window that mother nature has carved. We were in no mood to appreciate its beauty, however, because the snow was coming down fast and furious. It had been my experience that if a guy rode around to the back side of these red rock cliffs he could get in out of the weather a bit. With that hope, we investigated the back. Sure enough, there was a pocket behind it about eight feet deep. There was just enough room to

74

spread out the gear along this protected ledge and get in under it ourselves. "Have to clean out this cactus and chico brush, though," said Luke.

"Sure enough," I replied. "Sweep out these bones too. Coyotes and pack rats have had their dens and nests here before us." I felt a little like we had invaded somebody's tomb.

One of Utah's natural wonders: Looking Glass Rock.

A Good Town
With a Bad Memory

Moab, Utah turned out to be both good and bad for us. It's a real quiet little town. Their early prosperity was due to prospectors finding uranium, oil and potash in the area. Today, uranium mining, tourism and ranching are the main activities. At one time it was a favorite target for Indian raids. In fact, the Indian War south of Moab in 1921 was the last one in the United States, we were told. Chief Poke and Posey were Piautes who were dissatisfied with the treatment from the whites.

Here we were 30 days into the trip and almost celebrities. Reporters stopped us just out of Moab and tied up a couple of hours taking pictures. They had us pose for all sorts of shots. Then they wanted me to sign a release so they could use the pictures they took in different advertisements. "No way!" I told them, angry about the wasted time.

In Moab we were greeted by Mr. Price, the exalted ruler of the Elks Lodge. He furnished us with a vehicle and made arrangements for the stock to be boarded at the fairgrounds. Even reserved a fantastic room at the Inca Inn. The king-size bed sure beat sleeping on the hard, cold ground! After a welcome shower, I headed for the Lodge.

They had a hot card game going and I picked up a few dollars. There was a bunch of gals running in and out. Got lined up with one, so I didn't spend much time at the Lodge after that. I swear this little gal could charm the lard off a hog. She took me to see a little old lady, Bertha Murphy, who was celebrating her 101st birthday. The old lady was so excited about meeting me and hearing about our trip.

This seemed a good place to lay over a day and give the stock a rest. Met a lot of old timers and found out we were just two days away from Green River, Utah where the Wild Bunch had stayed. It was kind of exciting to be in the land where the gang used to hang out. Robbers Roost Ranch was just south of Green River. Course the outlaws didn't broadcast their locations and everybody had a different story of just where who had been and when. They all seemed to agree, though, that Butch Cassidy had indeed called the area home at one time.

Talked to one guy whose father was a frontier doctor. Outlaws stole his horse, so he just saddled another one and rode right down into Robbers Roost. Got his horse and took him home and nobody said a word to him.

Met an outfitter name of Mike who said his was kind of a glamour business in the minds of young kids. "Some of my employees are pretty good hands," he said. "I tell 'em out front, now look we don't pay much, but we sure work your ass off." That way we start 'em off right. Otherwise they think it's all floatin' down a river and lolligaggin' around. They forget you gotta pack and unpack." I sure knew all about that! If you didn't get something tied on right, it wouldn't ride for long.

"How many employees you run a season?" I asked.

"Typically 20. And I got 17 vehicles. Been doin' it for 12 years, both jet boats and canoe trips."

"Damn pretty country to run through," I observed. "Looks like a lot of antelope around these parts."

"Right. Damn near everything you ever heard of is here. Bear, buffalo, deer. My dad came west in 1874 behind a herd of cows. I know this country like the palm of my hand. You hittin' us at a bad time, though. Lot of snow and bad weather lately."

"Tell me about it!"

And the weather didn't improve any as we left Moab two days later. In fact, we got about 20 miles out and a cop came along and shut us down. Said we couldn't be on the highway because the snow was so heavy the traffic couldn't see our pack train. I asked him to let Mr. Price know about our predicament, then led the horses over a little ridge to set up a camp of sorts. The wet snow penetrated everything. Fortunately, Mr. Price arrived soon with a couple of bales of hay for the horses and the invite of a warm bed in town for us. I felt sorry leaving Woof behind in all the snow. He was standing guard on a ridge as we drove off and seemed resigned to staying behind.

It was into the second day before the wind stopped howling and the snow abated. I was as itchy to be on our way as a cow with her tits in a thistle. But when we returned to camp, a ghastly scene awaited me. I found Woof three-forths covered with snow, a gunshot wound through his head. He probably was mistaken for a coyote standing on that ridge in the snowstorm. My throat had a lump the size of a goose egg in it. My eyes stung. It was all the harder because *he* had chosen *me*. He was just a big ole pup, but he was a hell of a dog. Loyal to the end.

My inner gloom matched the bleak sky as I went about breaking camp. Trashy was in hobbles. As I caught hold of the hobble strap, she leaned around and got my hat in her teeth and bit a big chunk out of it. I was in a bad mood anyway because of Woof—and her antics made me down right mad. I jumped up and grabbed a willow stick and took after her. Trashy started hopping away through three feet of snow.

Meantime, Luke was holding the rope and trying to keep up with her. I continued chasing her, cussing all the time. Somehow she was able to negotiate the deep snow in spite of her hobbles. Luke wasn't so lucky. He fell down and didn't let go. It had the effect of a snow plow; the ole snow sprayed out both sides of him. When he finally thought to let go, I was laughing so hard I couldn't even catch my breath . . . let alone my mule.

"But, Sir, I Didn't Know It Was a Missile Range!"

Luke saw no humor in the situation. He had met a little lady back in Moab he claimed was "delicate as a dandelion puff." He decided to spend a few days with her and catch up with me later. I had to personally chuckle about the idea of a dandelion puff and a snow plow getting together, but I wisely kept these thoughts to myself as he gathered up his personal gear. My aim was to get to Alaska as quick as I could.

To that end, folks in Moab had told me about some country I could cut across and save several miles, so I took off in that direction. Noticed signs that said "Restricted Area—Missile Range" but figured they weren't in effect now or the people wouldn't have told me to go through there. Just to be on the safe side, I traveled along under big power lines that marched across the area. If they had any mind to shoot missiles, it sure wouldn't be into power lines. That was about all there was. No grass, no nothing; just bare ground, patches of snow and power poles. And the wind blowing with a 30 mph headwind. It was barren, lonely and cold. I kept standing up in my stirrups to keep my

81

feet warm and the blood circulating.

I knew this was going to be a long, difficult haul for the animals, so when I had run out of groceries in Moab, I hadn't restocked, figuring the extra weight would be a burden for them. I knew I'd be alright for a couple of days. But now I was getting worried. I hadn't seen a rabbit or a duck or a prairie dog . . . nothing to shoot and eat. My belly was beginning to grumble loudly. I did find a little peanut butter and honey in the bottom of the saddlebag and ate that.

The snow never seemed to quit, but the tent helped a little.

For the next four days I endured excruciating cold. It was snowed in at one point for 2½ days. And it got to 10° below zero with a head wind! My lips were cracked and bleeding. My ears, hands and feet were a constant source of concern since they had been frozen before. I wanted to turn back. But I was at the point of no return. It was too far back to Moab, so I might as well go on into Green River . . . if I could. My only food was now the Omalene I had taken for the horses. I boiled it up and made a hot oatmeal out of it and put on the last of the honey. It was fortified with vitamins and iron, so that helped, I guess. Figured what was good for my horses was good for me too. But I sure would have taken kindly to a steak!

A cold and lonely ride across the Green River Missile Range.

Mula, Red, Joanne, Trashy and Freckles pause to rest
and search for food.

Of course, I knew by now that the "shortcut" didn't exist. I was lost in the middle of this damn missile range without another human being within only God-knew-how many miles. I had experienced solitude before. Then it had been full of contentment; a well in which I dipped for refreshment of my soul. This was different. There was a hopelessness about this that chilled my bones! It felt even worse than the cruel wind and cold. God, how I wanted to quit! To just be home in my warm bed with a full belly. I had felt this way once before in my life. That was in Nam when we were giving air gun support to ground troops.

It was strictly a volunteer unit. We flew helicopter gunships. The life expectancy was 90 days and there was no rank, everybody was equal. I flew in boots, denim shirt and jeans and they called me "Cowboy." The only way to survive the pressure between runs was to dream you were somewhere else.

The V.C. had stolen 50 caliber machine guns and mounted them in the mountains, which were called the Three Sisters, below the Delta on the boundary line of South Viet Nam and Cambodia. We had to fly below 300 feet because if we dropped down that low they couldn't get us with their cross fire. From 300 to 800 feet they could hear us coming and shoot us out of the air. Out of nine ships, we had only three left within a week.

One morning about eight o'clock my machine gunner was wounded. We flew him back to the fuel base, took him to the dispensary, refueled and rearmed, and went out again. The crew kidded me on the way out: "Just another shootout like the OK Corral." That afternoon back at Three Sisters, I was flying with my copilot and good friend, Captain Bronson. All of a sudden Bronson took a round that came through the window, circled inside his new "bullet-proof" flight helmet and severed his jugular vein. I felt like my insides had been ripped out. There was nothing I could do but watch the guy bleed to death. I took the ship home with the gory mess that had been my friend by my side. "What the hell was I doing here?" I thought . . . and my mind escaped. I was riding horseback and pulling a pack string bound from the Mexican border, North to Alaska . . .

The following days I was really spooked. Everybody with a

short time before going home was getting it. The captain had had 60 days. I had 90! One morning Jerry Gotsy took a round. Jerry had been like a big brother to me. When it happened my copter became that horse . . .

Then it appeared *my* number was up. That afternoon my copter was knocked out from under me. Would the Cong get to me before our rescue ship did? I thought of a long ride, never made before . . . By golly, I'd do it! I was still laying the plans when a sister copter swooped down and picked me up. I'd always wanted to be first at doing something. And there was no record of anyone making the journey on horseback from Mexico to Alaska in one season . . .

When the weary horses, mules and I crested the hill we had been climbing, a strange sight met my eyes. There below, spread out for a mile in every direction it seemed, was the Green River Missile Base. Even though it was surrounded by a six-foot-high barbed wire fence, it was a truly welcome sight!

As we headed down the hill, here came an Army jeep going 90 mph. The driver screeched to a halt and began chewing my butt out. 'Who was I? Where was I going? What did I think I was doing? This was a restricted area. I couldn't be here. I had to turn around and go back!'

Needless to say, I wasn't about to turn around and go back. After he simmered down a little and we talked, I found out I was only five miles out of Green River. I promptly explained to him that it would be foolish for me to turn around and go back 50 or 60 miles, when I only had to go five miles in the other direction to be off the base. Finally he got his head out of the clouds and agreed with my logic. But he still didn't trust me. The devil escorted the stock and me all the way out so I wouldn't detour and take pictures or anything. Little did he know . . . food and warmth were much higher on my list of priorities than picture-taking!

By the time I reached Green River things were looking better. I got inside a coffee shop and poured some hot brew in me and was raring to go again within an hour's time. People suggested I stay at the stockyards in Green River. I put up for the night in a haystack there and had plenty of feed for the livestock and a good dinner for me.

While I had been getting my coffee, an old timer had given me some advice on how I could make up some of the time I'd lost coming across the missile range. I was leary of another "shortcut," but he seemed very sure of himself, so I decided to give it a try.

Well . . . we hit an area where flash floods had come through and had to detour around. The ground was still soft and muddy and real hard on the horses. They lost three shoes in the process. With the tough going, I made only 18 miles that day. The stock was worn out from going up and down hills and through mud. I shot a rabbit and made a stew for supper, then crawled in the sack about 6:30 because of the cold. Of course, I lost time again. The next day I pushed hard and did almost 50 miles just to get out of there and back on some sort of schedule.

While I was going along the next day, Luke caught up with me. "How's it goin'?" I asked.

"That was some little lady!" he exclaimed, then inquired what I had been up to. I told him not to ask! We were shooting the breeze when here came a bunch of reporters. They flocked around us and one said, "Where did you find the body?"

Luke and I stared at each other and squirmed nervously in our saddles. "Just what do you mean?" I asked.

"The body. You know, the guy who was shot through the head and dumped out."

"You guys are crazy! I don't know anything about any body!" As we talked, it came out that a man had been found around where we had just come through. Somehow the news media got the idea that we had found the remains. When they learned that wasn't the case, they had questions of a different nature all about our trip. They were excited to meet the cowboys they had heard about.

At our campsite that night, we were short of drinking water. I went ahead and used some alkali water that I had seen the cows drinking. I boiled it and made coffee and we drank a little. That was a mistake. I'd no more gotten settled in my sleeping bag than mother nature called . . . and called . . . and called. When I pulled myself out in the morning it was with great effort. Luke seemed to have survived the tainted water with no ill effects, so he did most of the breaking of camp.

It was that day I discovered how impossible it is to travel with diarrhea. I'd have to stop about every 30 minutes and hunt up a tree. This proved especially difficult. Not that there weren't any trees. But now that I was a celebrity, whenever people would see the pack train stopped, they took that as a personal invitation for them to stop their cars, get out and talk with me. I'd no more dismount and squat, then here would come some curious person wandering over to visit!

Going into Price a fella stopped by and gave us a 100-pound bag of feed pellets. This proved both a blessing and a curse. When you're short on cash and food, you don't look a gift horse (if you'll excuse the expression) in the mouth. On the other hand, another 100 pounds really put an extra load on the stock. I reasoned they would eat up their burden in short order, however, so we re-distributed the gear and added the sack of pellets.

Price, Utah was a good stop. We had a police escort all the way through town. There had been enough media by now that people recognized us most everywhere we went. The Mission Inn, where we stayed, even had a "welcome" sign up on the marquee. After checking in and soaking under a hot shower, I had dinner and a party at their nice little Elks Lodge. Everybody made me feel right welcome. They told me how Price is famous for the dinosaurs that stalked there in remote times. Fossil hounds come there today to hunt for traces of the ancient creatures.

My coat was really dirty, so an Elk brother—who owned a cleaners—volunteered to get it dry cleaned and said he'd catch up with me to bring it back. As it had turned to shortsleeve weather, that sounded like a good idea.

Tragedy Strikes
On Soldier's Summit

As we took off over Soldier's Summit, storm clouds were gathering ahead. I gave an involuntary shiver thinking of meeting that storm without a coat for protection. But I needn't have worried. A few miles further, here came the brother with my clean coat and wishes for a safe and exciting trip.

The going was tricky. Because the road was such a narrow highway, I decided it would be best to travel on the outside of the guard rail. That way we were less likely to be struck by traffic. The snow plows had scraped the snow off the road and it was packed and icy on the side where our train was traveling. We were getting along fine until we came to a narrow, slick spot. The horses started to slip.

"Help me get 'em over the guard rail. Quick!" I shouted to Luke. We got Joanne and Red over okay. Then we went back for Trashy. It was harder to entice her over, but we finally succeeded.

Mula, however, was a different story. The guard rail was almost three feet high and she was loaded pretty heavy. She was afraid. We would pull—and the mule would balk, frightened that she would fall. We had almost coaxed her over when she lost her footing and went tumbling down the canyon wall.

"Oh, my God! Mula!" It was a drop of 150 feet. As soon as she fell and started going down, she just quit . . . didn't move . . . didn't fight . . . nothing . . . just hung there with the pack boxes looped on her. I didn't know whether she was dead—or smart. I did know I couldn't get her back up. Reluctantly I dropped the pannier boxes to the bottom of the canyon, then dallied and tied off the rope on Joanne. "Get those tourists to help hold Joanne!" I yelled at Luke. By now passersby had traffic stopped both ways. Joanne was out in the middle of the road, straining on the rope for all she was worth. Then little by little, a step back at a time, the paint mare skidded Mula up the side of the canyon and to the guard rail. She lay on her side. I was watching intently, trying to decide if Mula was dead or alive.

When she thought she could get her footing, up the mule jumped and went gladly over the rail. "I'll be damned," beamed Luke. "She don't seem hurt none at all." The slide down on the ice and snow hadn't even bruised her. She was one smart mule! I wouldn't have been able to hold her if she had been fighting when she was over the side and she seemed to sense that.

"Well, now that we've got her up safe, I'm goin' after the panniers," I said. The people in the first car got the traffic moving and I tied ropes to the guard rail. Then I shimmied down the ropes, located the panniers and tied the rope to them. People from the cars hauled the pack boxes up to the top. I came up hand-over-hand and very out of breath. We got Mula re-packed amidst much picture-taking, offers of help and good-natured kidding.

It was cold and miserable laboring over Soldier's Summit. A highway patrolman stopped and asked if there was anything he could get for us.

"Just some snake bite medicine," I joked. He waved and headed off.

About an hour later, here came the highway patrolman again with a fifth of Seagrams VO. "Drinkin' and drivin's no good, but drinkin' and ridin's okay, eh," I said with a grateful grin.

"Cold as it is, figured you boys needed something to get your blood circulating," he replied. "You see that coal mine aways back?" I remembered passing an expanse where the earth had been cut and mutilated. "Carbon production's vital to this area. The main thrust began when the Denver and Rio Grande Railroad was cut through from Colorado to Salt Lake City in '83. Bet you wouldn't mind sitting by a nice coal fire now."

"Sure wouldn't," I agreed.

A pause for "R & R" atop stormy Soldier's Summit.

Just outside of Tucker it was spitting snow and cold. The wind whipped fiercely. My full beard was caked with ice, so were my eyelashes and hair, which by now was overly long. We rode by a nice ranch house with corrals and barn, but no stock around.

"Think I'll ask to stay overnight here," I told Luke, turning Joanne into the driveway. A woman answered my knock. "Afternoon, Ma'am, I'd like to ask permission for us to spend the night in your barn. We'll be glad to clean it out or do some other chore as payment."

"No. Just git off my place," she snarled.

"But I don't understand," I replied, shocked. This was the first encounter I'd had with bad hospitality. This woman was plain snotty. Wouldn't even talk to me.

"Nothin' to understand. Just go!"

"Whew! What a bitch," Luke said, overhearing our conversation.

"Maybe she just had a fight with her old man."

"Or maybe she ain't got one and that's her problem," Luke chuckled. "Anyway, it's a cinch we ain't staying here tonight."

A little further up we found some old railroad stock pens about a 100 yards off the road. Looked like they hadn't been used in about 20 years. The gate was open so we went on in, tramping over snow a foot and a half deep. We made camp on top of it and wrapped up in a tarp. It was an awful night. How I looked forward to sunshiny days and green grass!

Escapades In
The Salt Lake Valley

After leaving Tucker we had a long day down to Provo. The paint mare had developed a big sore under the saddle bags. Scalded it seemed. "Tough to imagine her gettin' a scald, cold as it's been. Awful touchy of her," I said, patting the neck of the horse I'd come to love and depend on so. "When we get into Provo we'll get some foam rubber or gauze to make it easier for you ole girl."

Provo was surrounded on three sides by majestic mountains. Her west was hemmed by Salt Lake Utah. Her floor was covered by six inches of snow! A ceiling of clouds hung suspended overhead. That was a real blow! I'd figured on bad weather from El Paso to Provo, but I'd counted on "green grass and clear sailing" once we hit the Salt Lake Valley. This was damn unusual for mid March. I'd seen grassy meadows and wildflowers through this section this time of year before. How I wanted it to be that way now! I'd had enough snow and wind and rain to last a lifetime! You had to be tough as a warehouse rat to stand the constant cold.

Had a heck of a time getting into Provo where I knew the Elks had a Lodge and riding stable. We went several extra miles down around a power plant by mistake. Finally met a man who seemed to know what he was talking about. He told us how to get there. But what would work for a motorist proved a real obstacle course for us.

A snow laden Salt Lake Valley. (My green grass and clear sailing!)

We hit Provo about five in the afternoon. It was rush hour. Making any headway was almost impossible. In addition to the normally heavy traffic, we caused our own traffic jams as people stopped and stared at us. This caused more problems. The livestock hadn't seen that many cars and trucks before. They were skitterish and wouldn't line out properly. They all wanted to huddle up around me and the lead horse for security.

I decided one solution might be to get off the main drag. Finding a side street that led in the right direction, we escaped to relative peace and quiet. It left much to be desired, however. After going about 12 blocks, it was obvious we were riding in circles; the street had wound around and no longer paralleled the main drag.

Eventually we found the Elks Club, got the animals quartered and learned they had arranged lodging for me. That was a happy surprise 'cause I desperately longed for a shower and a comfortable bed . . . and our money was running dangerously low. They put me up on the 13th floor of the Golden Spike,

94

which was a Travelodge. I no more than checked in when young ladies came running in and out to meet the "celebrity." Then some Elks came by and gathered me up and off we went to the Lodge for dancing. They had quite a poker game going too and they kept trying to get me to play. I couldn't afford to lose the little money I had left, so I told them I couldn't.

A guy was sitting there with a stack of chips in front of him. He had been losing his shirt from what I'd seen. "Come over here and play my chips," he said, gesturing to me. "I'm going to take a break." So I sat down about midnight, using his money, and went to town. He knew what he had when he left; just sat at the bar and watched me play hour after hour. Never did ask to get back in the game, just backed off and let me play. When the game ended that night he gave me a share of what I had made. It was $120. Yep, the crap table has always been good to me!

When we left Provo they made arrangements for off-duty officers to provide us with a police escort. The officers did it on their own time with no extra pay. Great guys. We went a whopping four mph! They turned on their lights and one car got in front and another brought up the rear. At intersections they would put a police car at the cross streets with lights flashing to hold up all traffic.

"This sure makes it easier in some ways," I remarked.

"Yep. With this here police escort all those poor folks who want an autograph have to go without. Ain't easy to stop a police parade," Luke said in a giddy and prideful voice.

Our trip was being touted in every paper by now and we were often asked to appear on radio and TV. It was impossible to get much privacy. In fact, I had to stop and spend the night in each Elks Lodge in the area. Sometimes I only made 10 miles a day through that region because I had to stop so often. It was exhausting! Each place we went I'd pick up a new group of people who wanted to hear the whole story. Then they would pass the hat or buy us drinks or give me a bottle to take along. It was one long round of storytelling and partying. I ended up with so many bottles of hooch, I had to ship some home!

Salt Lake City was something else. We were the first live-stock to hit the streets of Salt Lake in 50 years. That meant, in addition to the curiosity, there was a lot of hassle because animals were where animals weren't supposed to be. As soon as they heard we were approaching downtown they broke traffic with police cars. Then along came four guys on motorcycles.

We have a police escort through downtown Salt Lake City, Utah.

Well, the old gray mule had been chased by motorcycles back in Colorado. She was deathly afraid of them. When the police escort gave way to the bikes, she panicked and started spinning around the paint mule like a button on the outhouse door! Of course, the pack she carried splattered all over the pavement—right smack in the middle of town, strewing junk across two lanes of traffic. My face turned the color of a ripe tomato. Here I was supposed to be a better cowboy than most anybody, and I couldn't even control my mule! Everybody—except me—had a big laugh over it.

The wreck managed to make me 30 minutes late for a meeting with the governor. They had bussed in a bunch of school kids to see the pack train and talk with me. Going up the capitol steps I had the saddlebags so bulging with whiskey bottles that necks jutted out in several places. A patrolman rode up on his motorcycle and said, "Son, you'd better push those whiskey bottles down in there. That won't look very good in the pictures with the kids and the governor." So I pushed and juggled and shoved, but they simply wouldn't all go down. My only alternative was to thrust three of them into the astonished patrolmen's hands and say, "Drink hearty!" Then we were led in to meet Governor Rampton, had our photographs taken, posed for the kiddies and ducked out the back way.

Again, a police escort met us at the back of the capitol building and escorted us through town towards Ogden. We put up there at the fairgrounds for the night.

From Ogden we went on into Brigham City. That's where the two railroads converge and there's a golden spike. A man came out and met me as I was going through town and told me to stop down aways at the mall. Said he wanted to talk to me. I was in a hurry and just plain tired. Not very hospitable. I wanted to get out away from crowds.

When I got to the mall, there were TV cameras set up, people milling all over and that same man again. Come to fine out, he was the mayor pro-tem, Dale Baron. He was as gracious as I had been rude and presented me with an imitation gold commemorative coin and good wishes. The TV cameras whirled and once again we were captured for the five o'clock news.

They have a little racetrack at Brigham and I knew one of the guys who worked there. He and his buddies all wanted me to stay and swap stories with them, but I couldn't because the Elks Lodge was having a big feast and you-know-who was the guest of honor. To be truthful, I'd have rather spent the evening with the racetrack hands where I could have excused myself and gotten some sack time when I was tired.

I couldn't really complain though. While the weather had been hell, I left the Salt Lake Valley with an extra $400 of donations and poker money in my pocket!

Headin' for
the Cutter Horse Races

On the Utah-Idaho border, at Washaki, I learned they had cutter finals coming up that weekend in Pocatello.

"Jus' what the hell is that?" inquired Luke.

"That's chariot races. Real excitin'! Ivan Ashman's president of the Cutter Race Association. Why, I used to train horses for him in Arizona. I even won a derby for him, racin' a horse called Takeadeck. But I hadn't ever met the man when it happened."

"That's kinda strange."

"Oh, he was a multimillionaire. Had lots of trainers. I wondered who the little guy was in the "win" picture with us, but none of the barn crew knew either, so I kinda forgot about it. Then about a half hour later I was back in the stable cooling the horse off and the little man came in and started askin' all kinds of questions about the horse. He wanted to know where I'd got him, who I'd got him from and so on. Then he said, 'Oh, by the way, 'I'm Ivan Ashman.' Sure surprised the hell out of me. By the time we were through I was as wound up as a corkscrew."

"He made ya nervous?"

"Hell, no. He took me out and wined and dined me. It was just that he was such a rich old dude and had so many good horses."

"Maybe he's got some to spare now," said Luke. "We could

sure use some fresh stock."

"Pocatello here we come!"

At Arimo we stayed the night, then swung off the highway to make better time getting to the races.

My enthusiasm was somewhat dampened by the weather, however. Just to be different, there was wind swirling around us and snow drifting down when we got there. It was the Northwestern National Finals and dozens of two, three and four-year-old teams were prancing around. Strangely enough there was no official betting and no money for the winners, just trophies. Yet there were teams present worth more than $50,000. During one race there was a horrendous wreck when the driver lost control of his team and they raced along an embankment. They got too close to the edge and dropped one chariot wheel over the side. The horses shrieked in pain as they and the chariot tumbled end-over-end down onto the course.

The Elks Lodge in Pocatello had a completely different bunch of people than any of the members I'd met before. They were friendly, but sort of uppity. You had to have on a suit and tie to even get in the club. Of course, they frowned on my bluejeans. I felt sort of out-of-place. I did meet a saddlemaker there who told me to stop by. The next morning I got some horseshoes, scrap leather and odds and ends to make harness repairs. I carried a leather awl and had used it several times to repair tack by the light of a campfire.

We stayed in Pocatello for three days, putting the livestock up at the fairgrounds. I caught up with Mr. Ashman. We shot the breeze and he took me out to supper. But he had hit a rough streak and wasn't the generous man I'd known in Arizona. There were no horses from him to replace my tired stock, even though in his usual tradition, he'd walked off with the winning team at the races.

Talked to some folks who referred me to a horse trader from back East, name of Cheyenne Kid. They told me I could find him in a nearby town, Sterling. Sure enough he was there and so was a big bay . . . a spunky, strong-willed horse. I traded my

100

sorrel for him.

That night just out of Blackfoot, Idaho, we encountered some Indian problems. A rancher had given us permission to put up our horses in his corral. Damned if the Blackfoot Indians didn't come and let them all out! Turned every last one of them loose. The dog raised so much cain that the rancher's wife called the Elks Lodge where I was playing cards to tell me what was going on. I was out chasing horses 'til daylight. It was lucky I caught up with all of them because the Indians would have claimed as theirs any I missed. That's one way to increase your herd!

Idaho Falls was a downright hospitable place. We were met by men from the Chamber of Commerce and the Elks Lodge. One of their first questions was "What do you need?"

The soles on my old boots had cracked open from propping my feet up around campfires to keep warm. "Where can I get a pair of cheap boots?" I asked, whereupon they took me to a Tony Lama outlet store that sold seconds. Twenty minutes later I was the proud owner of a brand new pair of Tonys—on them! That night they introduced us to several young ladies and we went dancing and out on the town.

The humane society at Idaho Falls had heard that I'd lost my dog a while back, so they figured this was a good way to give a home to one of their charges. "Come to the animal shelter and pick one out," the director told me. Well, there was a mutt there that really took my fancy. We decided he must be part yellow lab, part blue mastiff and part St. Bernard. The big yellow-colored brute stood about three feet tall . . . and he was still a young dog. "Make a whale of a watchdog," I commented. When I told the staff I didn't know whether to put a lead shank on him or pack him, everybody laughed. They gave "old Yeller" three hours of schooling, after which he could hardly walk!

I put out the word with those traveling ahead that I would need a horse soon. People had called and alerted the main horse trader and he came out to sell me a horse as I rode into Roberts, Idaho. I hoped to trade off Red. He was broke out good now but was getting kind of sluggish.

This fella had a big good-looking bay. A stout gelding, eight or nine-years-old and used to mountain riding. "I'll take $800 fer 'im," the trader told me.

"No, way!" was my reply. Livestock was already costing me a fortune. I would buy an animal fat and sturdy and it would be slimmed down and tired when I went to sell it, so I always traded at a loss. But $800 was just out of my bracket, even though I liked the horse.

Riding along a road headed for Salmon, we met a farm family. They hailed us to stop, then brought out fried chicken, light bread fresh out of the oven and some coffee. As we chatted over supper the farmer said, "Wish I'd a knowd you was comin' through here. Had a great horse and jus sold him. Was a stout gelding. I'd a give him to you. Exactly what ya need. But this here horse trader came out and bought him jus' yesterday. Paid me $150 fer him."

The kindly farmer nearly had a heart attack when he heard how much the horse trader was trying to re-sell his horse for!

The next day it was cold and windy and drizzling rain. Midafternoon we rode into a town called Mud Lake. It consisted of a bar, grocery store and cafe, a couple of houses, a trailer and a few trees. I tied my lead horse to a tree and went in to have some coffee. Their coffee was so strong it could have leaped off the deep end of the Richter scale. While I was gingerly sipping a cup, this old gal stomped in just ranting and raving at us. Seems I had my horses tied to her tree and she felt I was trespassing. A guy down the counter took pity on us. "It's cold and you've traveled far enough today. Just take your stock down to the baseball field." He pointed us in the right direction, then glared at the woman.

The baseball field was all fenced and seemed an ideal place to put up the stock. We closed them in, then went back and had some supper. Things turned into a party and most of the couple of dozen town's inhabitants joined in. Later we got a ride back to the baseball field and put our bedrolls and tack in the dugout, then settled down for the night.

About two o'clock Old Yeller started carrying on something fierce. I got up and pulled on a coat to see what was going on. A couple of kids had opened the front gate and turned all our stock loose! They were heading in various directions. I grabbed a flashlight and took off after them. Trashy is a bugger to catch. I wound up wasting the whole day there rounding them all up. Everybody in the little community felt bad.

Trashy and the "board of education."

Out of Mud Lake it's a long, straight ride. Looks like it goes forever. My lousy luck was still holding. I could see a snowstorm coming, so we pulled off to set up camp before it hit. It was a big, black front, coming closer all the time. That night about a foot of snow dumped on us. It was as welcome as ants at a picnic.

The next day was still miserable. A gentleman stopped us on the road to invite us to spend the night with him and his wife. Said his ranch house was about a mile away and it would get us out of the weather. Turned out his sense of distance wasn't too good. Their ranch house was more like three miles away instead of the one mile he had proclaimed. There was a foot and a half of snow everywhere.

Deserted road near Leadore, Idaho.

"Know of a shortcut from here into Leadore," he explained that evening. "It'll cut off several miles." Taking his advice, we headed in that direction the following morning. But it wasn't to be. The snow was so deep we had to back off and return to his ranch to spend another night. Twelve hours later we left again, this time sticking to the road where snow plows had been at work. We headed over Gilmore Divide. There was about five feet of snow on the level. In some places it had drifted into towering white walls.

Leadore was our next stop. It was a nice little community of just over 100. Some folks told me we could stay in an old deserted homesteaders house. Here there were only small patches of snow and the grass was starting to green up. It was good grazing. There was even a running stream out back with fish eight to 10 inches long. But I couldn't get 'em to bite to save me. Locals said to use salmon eggs, but those buggers weren't interested in my salmon eggs, that was for sure. That's when I found out fishing with heavy weights is good. Twelve gauge shotgun slugs are perfect! You shoot in the water and they float up to the top and you have fish for supper! We had a heck of a mess of fish that night.

Actually I'd been very lucky all along the trip. Nobody ever expected me to have a fishing or hunting license. Just so long as we only took what we could use, nobody said a thing.

Before we left town the principal asked us to come and talk to the kids, so we got saddled up and rode over to the grade school. The kid's eyes were as big as sunflowers. They hung on every word we said and asked more questions than a rabbit has babies.

Riding along that afternoon we past Fort Lemhi. It was a religious settlement of Mormon missionaries at one time. Today some of the old ditches are still in use. In one area we could detect part of an old adobe mission wall still standing.

That night we spent at a ranch in Tendoy, Idaho, then rode on toward Salmon—halfway between the North Pole and the Equator. We passed a big sign proclaiming "45th parallel." At this point it was spitting snow again and very cold. I was beginning to wonder if we were ever going to get out of the cruel weather.

Sign near Salmon, Idaho.

When we pulled into Salmon I discovered that the Elks had planned a big dance in my honor. They told me to leave the

105

stock at the fairgrounds, then come on over. When I got to the Lodge everybody there was all dressed fancy for a formal dance. Here I was denim shirt, bluejeans, a couple of weeks worth of grime and smelling like a stable! Most embarrasing. But it didn't seem to make much difference to them. We whooped and hollered and danced 'til nearly dawn.

The next day Luke and I were following the river outside of Salmon. One place we paralleled the Lewis and Clark trail. The river had three-foot snowbanks on either side, but at this point I was bound and determined to take a bath. Two weeks of no washing was more than I could stand! So . . . I just pulled off my clothes and jumped in the Salmon River.

"Don't take long to git your bath when the water's running off a damn iceberg," I muttered. I had swam across the river, but since my clothes were on the other side, I had no choice but to swim back again so I could get dried off, dressed and warm again. While the cold water was a terrible shock to my system, I was in for an even bigger shock to come.

The Salmon River in Idaho.

One mighty cold bath tub!

A
Life and Death
Moment

On the way to Lost Trail Pass I shot two coyotes. Traded them to an outfitter who put us up for the night in a cabin he had at the crest of the pass. He was a big help. Told me things I was still doing wrong and how to pack the mules better. Even showed us how to throw a diamond hitch and gave us some tips on balancing the pack.

Going down the pass we saw several herd of deer and elk. Snowbanks were piled high along the fence on both sides of the road, making the clearance narrow. The jake brakes on the logging trucks were another problem. They are a compression brake that make a weird noise when you back off the gas. That scared the hell out of Mula. Everytime a trucker applied his brakes, I expected her to go into a rain dance. There was a surprising lot of traffic out anyway and that was unsettling to the animals.

Continuing on US 93 towards Hamilton, Montana, I could almost smell Canada on the wind. We were heading North and moving ever closer to our goal. Canadian geese were flying over in groups of eight to 10, headed North back up to cool country. They flew at treetop level, occasionally landing on some ponds across the river from us to rest and feed.

"Seems strange to have it 65°. I think we finally hit good weather," I said.

"Pretty country with them snowcaps and meadows all green with the cows out there," Luke replied.

"Yep. Now if I can just figure out what's botherin' Joanne, we'll be in good shape."

"She was straining yesterday. Couldn't take a pee. Maybe got kidney problems."

"Could be. The mules seem to be goin' downhill too. We'll have to give 'em some time to rest up soon or trade 'em off. Big bay's comin' along good. Really gettin' hard."

We were riding along commenting about the animals and countryside and minding our own business when we rounded a turn and here came a big red Olds barreling down the road . . . on the wrong side! The road was narrow and we were riding facing traffic. He was coming straight at me! Then he swerved, hit down into the bar ditch and went into circles, still heading right towards us, only now skidding sideways. We got over against the snowbanks and fence as far as we could, but there was really no place to go. The livestock were excited and scared, snorting and pawing the ground. I felt trapped. Couldn't move fast enough to get to the other side of the road and get out of his way.

A few seconds later the Olds slid by sideways about five feet away. After he passed, the driver straightened out the car and went right on down the road. Didn't even bother to slow down to see if everything was okay.

When I climbed down off Joanne to check the stock, my knees felt like jello. I'd had some close brushes with death in Nam, but this fit right up there with the worst of them. Luke was also shaken up but we decided the smartest thing to do was make a big push and get off this damn narrow, dangerous stretch of highway as quickly as possible. It was a hard ride into Hamilton.

They had a great Elks Lodge there. Gambling setup with roulette wheels, dice games, card games, you name it and they had it. Met a good looking gal there and she introduced me to her brother who said I could stay at his place.

"Come on, honey, I'll show you where it is and we can put the stock up," she cooed. When we got there I started to unsaddle my horse and she grabbed hold of Trashy. She started jerking the mule around so she could get off the pack and unsaddle her.

"Best you just leave her," I told the gal. "She'll get you. She's a mean bugger sometimes."

"Oh, I'm an old hand at this. I can handle any mule," she said taking ahold of Trashy's halter and pulling her over to a cement slab.

Just then Trashy rared up and came down on her. The gal had on a tank top, no bra. Trashy came down on both sides of her head and caught the straps of her top with the backs of her horseshoes and just peeled that shirt clear down to her waist. Trashy took the gal's hide with it and knocked her flat on her butt. She sat down hard on the cement slab, still holding onto Trashy's lead shank, looked up at the mule and said, "Well, I'll be an SOB!"

The next day both her eyes were black and she was so sore she could hardly move.

I decided to let the stock rest some and to see if I could pick up some fresh horses. Had heard about a ranch called Marcus Daly Estates where they raised Hungarian cavalry horses. Marcus Daly was a copper king. He built these estates back when the copper rush was in full swing. There was a fabulous big mansion on the place. It was said to have 30 three-room suites, 30 bathrooms, 20 fireplaces and a huge trophy room. There was also a mile and a quarter race track. It had been the training quarters for the only Kentucky Derby winner ever to come out of the state of Montana . . . a horse by the name of Tamby. Daly built a big fancy building in honor of this horse and called it Tamby Hall.

The ranch was now owned by his grandaughter, the Countess Daly. She proved to be a sloppy, gray-haired, cantankerous old gal who had spent time in concentration camps. No doubt as a result of that experience, she now shunned the public and cherished her privacy. She begrudgingly introduced me to her foreman, Bud, and said I could look over the horses. Bud explained that the countess didn't believe in breaking anything until it was eight years old. Then he led me through the barns. There was some mighty beautiful horseflesh there! Tough, durable animals. Bud told me she never allowed pictures to be taken in the barns . . . but he obligingly turned his back when I pulled out my camera and took a few shots. He even took me into the trophy room

A carriage in one of the Marcus Daly Estate display rooms.

"The Countess owns 300 of the 500 Hungarian cavalry horses in the United States," Bud told me. "Only three other herds and none so big."

I had to admit several horses looked promising to me. But when we went back to talk to the Countess, she refused to sell or trade me even one.

"Must not be any good, or you'd give me one for publicity,"

I taunted.

With that she had the foreman show me to the gate, saying, "If he comes back, shoot him!"

Hungarian cavalry horses on the Marcus Daly Estate
in Hamilton, Montana.

Everybody had told me that when I hit Missoula, Montana I was sure to get a grand welcome. It was the Cowboy Town of the West, they said. What a hoax that was! Luke decided to take off on his own for a bit and I pulled into Missoula on April eighth after following along the wide, placid Bitteroot River. As usual, one of the first things I did was call the Elks Lodge. They knew absolutely nothing about me or the trip. I called the newspaper next. Zilch. The TV stations said they had no air time available. When I got to the fairgrounds where I planned to put up my stock for the night, they wouldn't let me in. There were empty stalls and pens, but they still wouldn't let me stay there. Why I don't know.

So I found a contractor's supply yard with a lot of trucks, sheetrock, wood, plumbing supplies and what have you. The owner said I could stay there the night. At least it had a man-proof fence around it and a gate that would shut. I turned the stock loose, then got a couple of bales of hay and grained them. After a bite to eat, I threw my bedroll in the back of a truck, Old Yeller crawled to the foot of it and laid down and we both went to sleep.

The next morning I picked up a money order at 10 o'clock, bought 50 pounds of feed and rode through Missoula and out the other end. Fella once told me, "If you're being run out of town, get in front of the crowd and make it look like a parade." Well, I had one hot damn parade going . . . they even "escorted" me out of town!

That night I camped at the "Y" where highways 93 and 90 meet, Luke rode in about sundown and we went to a little bar we'd seen along the road to have a couple of drinks.

Figure we'll hit the border about the 20th," I told Luke. "Need to pick up some time, though. Beginning to feel pressured. If we cross around the 20th, that'll give us three months to make the last half of the trip."

"Think we can do it in that?" Luke inquired.

"Hell, we better! I want to be back home in time for the Stampede. This first half the days are short and there's been a lot of towns. But North when we get into Canada and Alaska, there's not as many towns. Days are longer, so we can travel with more daylight."

When I went to sleep that night Old Yeller was snoozing on the foot of my sleeping bag. The next morning he was gone. Normally, he willingly stayed right there with me and the stock. Heading up 93 towards Arlee, my heart was heavy. It looked like I had lost another dog.

Paradise
Found

Everywhere you looked it was green and there were animals. Game was so abundant that in the space of one morning we saw deer and elk and even a herd of wild bison. For dinner that evening we dined on duck. There were geese and duck aplenty.

The next day out we made good time traveling along a ridge called the Mission Mountains. "Boy, you talk about pretty hills. Ain't never been nothing more pretty, all snowcapped and the sun ashining on 'em," said Luke drinking in their beauty. Aspen stood head to toe with stately pines.

We made camp in a draw with good grass for the horses. There were yellow wildflowers—like a tulip only bigger—blooming all over the place. A stream gurgled not 50 feet from our camp. Firewood was laying all around. There were inch and a half chunks and pieces up to three feet long. We went out and picked up a bunch and in 15 minutes had enough for a roaring fire without even having to chop it. The mosquitoes had started and yelping coyotes talked in the distance.

"Heard tell this is bear country," said Luke.

"They say grizzlies come out of the Mission Mountains and kill livestock."

"Hope to hell they stay away from us!"

As we drank coffee and talked I heard a grouse hollering and woodpeckers at work. An old cow bellered off a ways. We had the paint mare on a picket and the other horses running loose. They wouldn't leave as long as Joanne was there. Even the old mules were getting easy to catch now. Of course, they should have been by this time.

Joanne enjoys her grain while I repair tack.

"Did you know this used to be an Indian Reservation?" I asked. "Indians called the Mission Valley 'Place of Encirclement.' The government finally opened it up to let white settlers in. They staked themselves out some pretty little ranches."

"Sure did. This here's a sportsman's paradise," commented Luke.

"Yup. Just one beautiful dream valley. Talked to an old boy on the road. He said land's going for $800 an acre around here. Course that includes water 'n mineral rights. Hell, this place sure has plenty of water. If it's not a natural lake or stream, there's a spring bubblin' up somewheres near."

The next day's ride was one of the prettiest we'd had. Besides the lush natural terrain, wildlife was everywhere. That night we camped just outside of St. Ignatius at the base of the mountains about two miles off the highway. A guy had told me to go ahead

The Mission Valley north of Missoula, Montana.

Just crossed Lost Trail Pass into the beautiful Bitterroot Valley.

and make camp in his pasture. It was a beautiful spot, again with plenty of firewood and next to a creek. And it was far enough back from the road to keep away the public and let us and the stock rest and relax. We spent two lazy days there. The

117

grass was long and green and there were 100 acres or so fenced in. That meant the animals could all be loose to graze. Freckles had a wonderful time chasing prairie dogs and rabbits; then returning to us for praise when he was victorious.

A campsite overlooking the Bitterroot River by Victor, Montana.

When we went to leave in the morning, I stopped by the people's house to thank them for letting us stay in their pasture. We got to discussing my plans. When I told him I wanted to add another horse to the string to have an extra in Canada, he said have breakfast with him and his wife and daughter. Afterwards they were going into Kalispell and I was sure to find a good steed there. So, after pancakes and sausage, we headed the 100 miles to the big horse sale.

I picked up a pretty good palamino about seven years old. He'd been broke out and had lots of schooling, but he'd bucked a couple of old boys off lately so they didn't trust him. I paid a little above what the slaughterhouse would have: $380. That was a bit high for me, but it was the cheapest horse there that would meet my needs. Since he was a big yellow horse, I called him "Trigger." I left Trigger in Kalispell. There was no way to trailer him back and I wouldn't really need him before getting into Canada anyway.

The people dropped me off at Polson on their way home and Luke met me there with the pack string. We stayed at the fairgrounds. The Polson Elks Lodge put on a good feed and we met a couple of girls there who told us to stop by on our way out the next morning so they could get some pictures. Their house ended up being right on the edge of the lake and built high on stilts. It looked like a knobby-kneed kid with a big woolen hat pulled down over his ears. When I climbed up and walked in, the floors cracked and snapped like cooking popcorn. I was relieved to get on solid ground again!

On the way up to Flathead Lake, Freckles was ranging ahead of us when he spied a chipmunk. Darting across the road after the little creature, he came right into the path of an oncoming VW bus. The driver stopped and apologized for what wasn't really his fault. We dug a shallow grave, deposited the lifeless body, and continued on. Luke was very quiet the rest of the day.

"'You ever see a bison run?" I asked.

"Nope" came the reply.

An old Indian bison run near Flathead Lake.

119

"Well, take a gander over there," I said, pointing to a towering cliff that jutted out from a high meadow. "Indians used to run buffalo to their death across that meadow and over the cliff. It was an easy way to slaughter 'em." Luke was lost in his thoughts and not very interested in my story.

Flathead Lake and the famous Wild Horse Island.

When we got to Flathead Lake a bunch of loggers saw us coming and yelled—pointing to a little bar called Bud's Place—"If you'll come in, we'll buy you a beer." Feeling a need to break the somber mood, I winked at Luke and replied, "We'll come in if you'll hold the door open."

They swung the door wide and I rode Joanne through, tearing the hide off both my knees in the process! Luke was right behind me on the bay. Once we got inside, it was so small everybody had to leave so we could get the horses turned around to get them out again. Of course, before we could do that we had to consume that beer we'd been promised!

Met a reporter there who was real friendly, so we invited him to our campsite for breakfast the next morning. When he arrived, he said there was a photographer waiting back at Bud's

Place and they wanted to take pictures and so a story. The second time we *led* the horses in and mounted them inside. My scraped knees couldn't take another go-round. In one picture it looked like we were playing a game of pool and the horses were watching.

As we rode into Kalispell, the picture taken in the bar with the horses hit the front page. Couldn't ask for better publicity. What I could have asked for was to feel better. Don't know what it was that didn't set well with me, but I was sick! Folks had been stopping us to talk on the outskirts of Kalispell and I was so sick I was hardly civil.

We headed for the stockyards and I collapsed into my sleeping bag while Luke unsaddled the animals and got settled in.

That night I was feeling better and we met the president of the Chamber of Commerce, Brent Hall. He was a hell of a nice guy. Took us over to the Outlaw Inn and introduced us at the desk.

"These cowboy's are going to be staying here a few days," he told the desk clerk. "Anything they want . . . food, drinks, whatever, just put it on a tab." The gal at the desk, a shapely blonde, was all smiles. "Have to get to know that little lady," I told Luke going up to our rooms. It was one hell of a swanky place and the women we saw were just as classy.

The next day Brent took me downtown to a sporting goods store. "Got a fishing pole, Tom?" he asked. When I told him "yes" he said I'd better send it home because we were gonna get what I'd need in Canada. With that he whipped out one of their shopping carts and we started up one aisle and down another. He dumped a new rod and reel, flies, sinkers and other tackle into the basket. Seemed Brent definitely knew his way around fishing. Then he says, "Tom, your clothes are getting pretty well worn out. You'll need two or three new pairs of jeans, some shirts and so forth." He proceeded to put these items into the basket too.

I was getting mighty panicky. How the hell was I going to pay for all this stuff he thought I needed? At the checkout counter the cash register twinkled merrily. When the figure passed $300, I began to turn green. "Mary," Brent said to the cashier, "Make a list of this stuff and tell the boss to put it on my account. This cowboy's headed for Alaska and we're going to outfit him right!" I could hardly believe my ears. When I started to protest, he countered, "Hell, Tom, you're doing something really special. Wish I could do it myself. Give me the pleasure of having a little part in it." With that he asked Mary for a box so I could pack my old stuff and send it home. What he didn't know was that most of it was so worn out it wasn't even worth keeping!

Over at the Elks lodge everybody was extra friendly too. They chipped in and made arrangements to feed our stock while we were there. Then a couple of them took us to a nice supper club at Big Fork.

The Elks and Chamber had quite a schedule lined out for us. They also wanted us to attend a $100-a-plate breakfast for a John Melcher, who was running for the Senate. "Imagine a couple of cowpokes like us with all these hifalutin' people," I told Luke as we munched our steaks.

Kalispell turned out to be quite a stopping spot. Roy Stanley, who owned the local Chevrolet dealership, furnished me with a car and we had this wide open ticket at the Outlaw. As it worked out, we spent eight days there. Canada requires that your stock be inspected before crossing over into their country. They gave the horses and mules what's called a Coggins test. Damn thing took eight days to get back the results. But it's an important test, we were told, as there was a lot of swamp fever going around and they wanted to be careful.

During our stay we were invited to a fancy restaurant on Flathead Lake. "This has got to be one of the damndest prettiest places," Luke said surveying the vast lake. It spans 120,000 acres and is 128 miles around its rim. Wild Horse Island sits right in the middle. We loved it so much we went out there Easter Sunday.

Another day I had a date with a gal to take a run around the lake in our loaned Chevy. She'd looked mighty shiny the night before about two o'clock. In the harsh daylight, however, it was quite another story. After a brief drive, I dropped her off and Luke and I went dancing with two of the desk girls from the

Outlaw. "Was good to do some dancin' and get the rust off my belt buckle," I told Luke after we dropped off the girls. He said he planned on staying on awhile in Kalispell.

Over the eight days I got to be pretty good friends with Dick Walters, who owned a bar on the outskirts of town called the Finish Line. He told me to be sure and stop so they could get some pictures in front of the bar. So on the way out, I gathered up the stock, smiled for the cameras, then went in to have a parting drink with Dick. It was 9:30 in the morning. "Got a bottle of Yukon Jack here on the back bar I want you to taste, Tom. Damn stuff's 101 proof and tastes like licorice," he said pouring me a glass.

Started talking to a trucker about the route ahead. "Main problem's gonna be wolves," he said. "They got them big old gray timber wolves. And they're multiplying like the coyotes down in the lower 48."

"What do their pelts go for?" I inquired, sipping on another glass of Yukon Jack.

"Wolves up north in the winter go as high as $300. There's a lot of 'em up there all right, but most people don't have the guts to stay out the winter and trap 'em. You're in the middle of nowhere and people are scared." We swapped stories about wolves and grizzlies and felt like old friends before long.

I left at two that afternoon after killing the Yukon Jack. Headed up to Highway 93. There was a lot of traffic out. Most of it looked like it was coming at me double. I got right in the middle of the highway and fell off my horse! I'd fall off, get up, walk under Joanne's neck and catch hold of the saddlehorn and crawl on . . . only to fall off the other side. Pretty soon traffic was stopped both ways and the animals were strung out behind me. Finally some guy got out of his car and came over. "Cowboy, you'd better let me hold your horse," he said. "I'll get her to stand still so you can get on." Then he ran over to the other side to see that I didn't tumble off. With his help, we finally crossed the highway successfully.

Another three miles and I rode down an embankment—and fell off again. So I just made camp right there. That was easier said than done, however. When I went to unpack the stock and take the panniers off, I couldn't untie the damn knots! So I went to cutting ropes and dumping packs. On one cut I slashed the cinch and turned everything loose. Then I put out my sleeping bag and flopped down on top of it and was out.

I awoke about 4 a.m. There was three inches of snow on top of me and I was as cold as marble laying on top of that sleeping bag. Everything—including me—was soaked. And, of course, the stock had taken advantage of my carelessness the night before and was nowhere to be seen. It took about three hours to catch them all.

Going into Whitefish, Montana Luke caught up with me and we met a barber along with a doctor friend of his on the road who said we could sleep in his hay barn. He ambled in later that night, lit a pipe and started telling us how he had lost a pack string. "Had five head go over a ledge last year. Poor devils dropped almost a thousand feet off a cliff."

"That's touch luck. How'd it happen, Doc?"

"I had a green horse in the middle of the string and something spooked him. He got sideways, lost his footing and went off. They were all tied together going up a narrow trail and when he went off he dragged all five over the cliff. They hit on a bunch of rocks and ground up like hamburger. Tore the packs all to pieces."

"Them green horses 'll get ya every damn time," Luke put in.

"You know, there's no point in leading a horse that isn't packing a load, Tom. Tell you what. Let's scrounge from all of those torn up saddles I've got left and see if we can't come up with one good one for Trigger. That way you can distribute the load and make it easier on the other stock too."

"That's mighty nice of ya, Doc. Sure does make sense," I replied. The three of us spent the next couple of hours working on the lattigals and breast collar that was worn away. When we finished, Trigger had a right nice pack saddle.

Trigger was coming along pretty good himself. He was a rodeo horse, but wasn't bucking enough to stay on the circuit. Though he wasn't bucking right for competition, he was too wild for most people to consider for a saddle horse. He'd been leading fine and now I wanted to pack him a bit before I started riding him. Put a light pack on him that first day. "He's a little humpy, but now that I've learned how to put on a pack so's he can't buck it off, it's a lot better," I told Luke. Actually, he didn't offer much resistance and I knew it wouldn't be long before he'd carry a man.

The paint mare was doing much better where she was scalded. Now Trashy was acting up. "Crazy mule's been farting and coughing like she had the alfalfa heaves," observed Luke.

"But she hasn't had any alfalfa. Can't even get the damn thing to drink much water. I'm gonna give her some B-12, copper and iron and 10cc's of Combiotic. She'll either be better—or dead—by morning."

We made camp at a ranger station and put up in the ranger's corrals. They had been having a lot of trouble with grizzly we were told. I didn't sleep well that night as we didn't have any dog now to warn us of pending trouble. And trouble, we would soon learn, was only a few days away.

Part Two

Welcome
to Canada!

Luke decided to take off on his own for awhile and I went on into Eureka. I knew it wasn't an official livestock port to go into Canada, but it was the closest point and I was no friend of defeat. The border personnel told me I couldn't cross there because there was no vet. Said I had to go back across to Sweetgrass, Montana or to Eastport, Idaho to take the stock across. When they saw that I wasn't about to take no for an answer, they came up with an alternative solution. "You could call the vet at Eastport, I suppose, and set up an appointment for him to drive over here and inspect you across," one of them volunteered. That's exactly what I did. He couldn't come for four days though, so I had time to kill.

I learned that Eureka had first been settled in 1908. Then they called it Tobacco. Today its roads are choked with trucks carrying two-by-fours. Logging is their big industry. I found an old West hotel that rented rooms for four-and-a-half bucks a night! It was a typical oldtime hotel with the bath down the hall. But it was nice and clean and they changed the sheets every day. It felt great just to be in a soft bed with sheets after so many nights in a sleeping bag on the hard ground! In their coffee shop I met several nice Canadians. Seems they come to the U.S. to buy groceries just like some Americans go down to Mexico to shop.

Meanwhile I met a family with two young teenage girls. They were darlings and real interested in what I was doing. Each had a horse so I showed them how to clip up and groom their horses. Then I gave them some pointers on shoeing horses and shod both of their geldings. They were scheduled to be in a show the next week, so they were excited about being able to show their animals to the best advantage.

Of course, in the process of helping them, I also got acquainted with their parents. Their dad was the manager of a Eureka bank . . . a real stroke of luck! You see, to get into Canada you must have $17 a day in cash or travelers checks for every day you intend to be in that country. I had zip. And I knew I'd be in Canada 60 or 70 days! Fortunately, the girl's dad floated me a loan in travelers checks so I'd have them to present at the port of entry.

On May first the vet showed up. The girls cut school and rode to the border with me. I offered to unsaddle the stock so the vet could inspect them. He walked once round the horses and mules, then said, "Hell, son, they've made it this far. Must be pretty healthy. I'd get on 'em and ride if I were you." Next he looked at the health papers, made out another set, signed us off and thanked me. Then he crawled in his car and took off; didn't even charge me!

The border patrol made out some papers declaring the horses "Canadian citizens" so I could trade them off if I wanted to and get me a 90-day visa. I rode into Canada, sitting tall and proud on Joanne, with the other four in tow.

Camp that first night was about nine miles in. I was sitting quietly by a lake when some friends from Eureka came out with a couple of busted bales of hay and steaks. We ate supper and shot the bull and I paid back the travelers checks. It was raining like an old cow peeing on a flat rock when we sacked out about 10 o'clock. Woke about 1:30 and the horses were raising hell. It was still misting and blacker than the ace of spaces. Heard the goldangdest ruckus . . . snorting and stomping, and thundering hooves. Couldn't see a thing. It finally quieted down and we went back to bed.

Joanne & I at our first campsite in Canada.

The next morning I discovered I had unknowingly set up camp about a half mile from a garbage dump where black bears hung out! Mula had broken off her picket and Trashy had hobbled away. It took half a day to gather them up. A bear had chased Trigger, who ended up with a perfect claw mark on his hip where the bear swiped at him.

I took a shortcut the following day that cut off about 10 miles. At one point a Mountie stopped me and asked for the permit for my rifle. I got into a little town called Fernie at six and located some people who let me set up camp across from their house in a pasture. It was a seven-acre plot with a stream cutting across it. I was glad the horses had water and food because 100 pounds of feed went pretty fast with five animals gobbling it.

Trigger was doing pretty good as a saddle horse now. He didn't like spurs and got a notion to bounce a few times during the day, but he kept his head up and didn't do anything but raise his butt a little. Only time he really got stirred up was when I got a rope under his tail. I was putting salve on his hip where the bear caught him and it was healing fine.

Just outside Fort Steel, British Columbia I purchased another horse. Figured it was a good idea to have an extra animal as we were heading into less populated areas and I didn't know if I'd be able to get horses later on. She was a 14-hand sorrel mare thoroughbred not bad looking, but small.

Luke hitchhiked up to where I was and climbed out of a pickup cluching a newspaper. "Look here," he beamed, showing me a front page story about our ride. I'd been on the radio too. Everybody finally believed I was serious! And to top things off, the weather was now 45 to 50 degrees and we had green grass. Finally!

On the ride that day we saw lots of deer and elk. Noticed bear tracks too, but no bear yet. The sorrel mare proved to be a real loser. "You see that dang horse walkin' on the other horses' feet? Almost crippled Trigger and the bay." I decided since she was too little to ride for any length of time and lousy to handle, that I'd break her and sell her for a dude horse. "A few days on the trail will show her who's boss in a hurry," I said. "You know, I sorta wonder about Joanne. Usually after a week or so on the trail most horses draw up and get lean and hard. But she hasn't."

"Yeah. You'd think with the hard work, she's slim down," replied Luke.

"Oh, hell, there's only one answer for that. She's in foal! Otherwise she wouldn't have such a belly." The knowledge saddened me. Joanne was a whale of a horse and I had planned on finishing the trip with her. But I knew it would be too hard on a new baby to be on the road right away. Somewhere, down the road soon, Joanne and I would have to part.

At Fairmont Hot Springs we laid over a couple of days and fished in the Columbia Lake which is fed by the Columbia River. We had a ball catching salmon, greyling and pike. Used six and seven inch greyling for bait. Ate like kings. Drank pretty well too. We met the sons of the man who owns the hot springs and partied with them on honey wine and moonshine. Got to know

A reflection of the majestic mountains
shining in the Columbia Lake.

the whole crew there. What a bunch of characters!

When we made camp the next time, the whole Fairmont
Hot Springs crowd trooped up in a van to Radium Hot Springs
to see how far we had gone that day. They brought steaks and

This little bugger is only the bait!

groceries. We took the girls horseback riding and were so busy showing off that all the animals ended up loose. Dern things started backtracking towards home in the United States. Took about half a day to track them down and get them turned around. "Have a hell of a time goin' north to Alaska with all our stock trottin' south," I told Luke.

Overlooking Radium Hot Springs, British Columbia, Canada.

Getting Joanne's pack settled.

Thank God
For Park Rangers

Heading into Banff National Park, we came upon a guard shack at the park entrance. The gal told the head ranger that we were there and coming into the parks. Usually you have to seal all guns going through their national parks. The ranger didn't know I was within earshot when he responded to his associate. "Well, these stupid bloody Americans. They're stupid enough to try anything. If they're stupid enough to make it this far, they may be stupid enough to make it all the way, so let them go." The woman apologized for half an hour for his behavior. I felt real sorry for her having to work with somebody like that.

Twenty-seven miles further we came upon Kootenay Crossing and passed into Alberta. Here a ranger station was located. The ranger and his wife were from Amsterdam and both were photo buffs. Nice folks and they really enjoyed seeing the pictures we had taken.

"Been having quite a lot of trouble with bear lately, Tom. Just about every night," he told me. "It's a big sow and her cubs, so you fellas beware." We took him at his word. We camped *inside* the corral with the horses and kept a fire going all night to keep the bears out. I could tell they were near though from the restlessness of the stock.

There were lots of snowcapped peaks around us. The snow

Bow Summit leading towards Glacier National Park,
British Columbia, Canada.

Trying to dry out our clothes and bedroll
at the foot of Eisenhower peak.

erupted down the craggy mountain sides like white lava. Mt.
Assiniboine pass was closed to vehicle traffic. They'd had snow

slides and it was hazardous. We went over it anyway. It was snowing and foggy and damp. By the time we hit Eisenhower Junction, I had heavy tarps on the packs . . . and they were still soaking through. We made a camp of sorts. I found a dead tree still standing and chopped it down to make a fire. We used the fire to try and dry out ourselves and our bedrolls. It was a dismal camp!

A man stopped us along the road the next day and gave us $20, saying it was from the Canadian Elks. He said he'd contact the Jasper Elks and tell them to be on the lookout for us. Seemed people were hearing more about us. The man said our story was on the radio in Calgary and on the Saskatchewan TV news.

Later that day we made it to Lake Louise and went into a store to pick up a few groceries. Things were so damn high! We didn't buy much, just a can of beans, a ham and some crackers. The bill for our groceries came to $24. But the old boy gave them to us for a five dollar bill to help us out.

Going over the top of a glacier, close to 10,000 feet, it was so wet and cold my tarps froze and were useless. I saw lots of bighorn sheep and elk. Had to cut down a standing tree again for firewood. Thank God they don't retain the rain and snow like downed wood, or we never would have gotten a fire started.

In this area the forest service people would load up hay and grain from the park service horses' supply for me. All that was open was the road through the parks. Snow was stacked on both sides six to seven feet high. There was absolutely no place to get off the road and make camp. What the park rangers did was send up a snow plow to make a camp area for me. How 'bout that for service! They would either use an existing camp site or create one with the snow blower so we could get back off the road. Then they'd leave some bales of hay.

The game wardens and national park personnel were real good people. Not only would they go out of their way to establish a camping site for me, they never required any type of fishing or hunting license. I could shoot or catch what I could use at any time.

137

They would stop me in the morning and ask how far I expected to make it that day, so they would know where to make the next campsite. They knew the road ahead, of course, and told me what to expect.

We noticed in some of the campgrounds there were little shacks built. Stayed in one. "boy, look at that six-burner stove," exclaimed Luke.

"Even has a baking oven," I added. This is a real nice little deal to get in out of the weather . . . big table, windows on three sides and open on the other.

"The stove ain't worth a damn though," put in Luke. "Don't draw right."

Typical national forest shelter in Canada.

The stock was doing so-so. The bay horse had an eye that was a little cloudy where he accidentally got whacked with a rope we were tying. Luke had shod the mule and the sorrel mare. "Mula isn't leadin' very well, must be hurtin' somewheres," I told Luke.

"Hell, she's just tender-footed from the new shoes."

"Maybe. Anyway, think I'll cut back on the grain since

we've got a good supply of hay for awhile."

That day we made it from Mesquite Campground to Waterfall Campground, about 20 miles. We were down in a little valley next to a lake that had about a foot of ice on it. "Let's try some fishing," suggested Luke.

"Stream's runnin' kinda murky with snowmelt. But we can give it a try. Lake hasn't even started to thaw yet."

"Hell, guy back there at the ranger station told me the Glacier Lakes never do thaw out."

"True. And a lot of the lakes and rivers are full of glacier silt. Man, are they salty! The spring water's a little better but it still tastes mighty salty. 'Course we can catch drinkin' water out of the springs bubblin' up everywhere."

"The water sure is blue . . . almost turquoise . . . not washed out like the lakes and rivers we got back home. Hey, look at the sheep up there," yelled Luke, pointing up on the hillside. There was a fat ewe with a pair of lambs at her side and five more head grazed twenty yards further up. Most all the wildlife we saw were fat and healthy-looking.

"I saw a couple of moose today," I said.

"Me too. An' I seen some bear tracks again."

We kept fishing for a couple of hours with no luck, so we quit and settled for ham and beans for supper. The birds were chattering up a storm and a little later we heard an owl hoot. It didn't get dark now til 10 or 11 o'clock. Was real hard to get to sleep before the sun went down. This particular night we stayed up and I played the harmonica awhile. It was one of the prettiest sunsets I'd ever seen, reflecting on the lake and all. The big ball of red crept over the mountains some 11,000 feet high . . . and I thought too late to go grab my camera. I was plumb lost in the beauty of it.

Going up and down the grades into Jasper was hard on the stock. Trigger had developed a fistulous on his withers and kept coming up sore. It was like a big cyst. I knew from past experience it would swell up like a football, be sore and take about six months to heal. Such damn luck! On the way into

139

town there was a guy who saw Trigger and decided he just had to have that horse. Well, that fit into my plans just perfect! I told the guy the horse was a little sore, but he says, "Don't matter. I want him!"

When we got into the fairgrounds where I was to put up the stock, I decided to doctor Trigger, as the guy was coming to ride him in a couple of hours. Injected some bute for pain killer around the sore spot. Then I worked the swelling out. Trigger couldn't feel a thing. When the guy put a saddle on him and tried him out he said, "He don't look or act bad at all." With that he plunked $800 in my hand, led Trigger into a horse trailer and was off.

The Canadian Elks were real nice people. They gave us a whole house to ourselves for the two days we were in Jasper. Had four bedrooms, groceries, everything. The Canadian Elks proved not only friendly, but downright party-minded. While I had one beer, they drank a six-pack. Their beer is mellow and light with very little carbonation. It runs from 10 to 18 proof and most of them drink it like water.

My boots were in awful bad shape, so when I met a fella at the Elks lodge who said he was a shoemaker, I asked him if he could get them re-soled in time for me to get on the road again soon. He said sure; even loaned me a pair of tennis shoes to wear in the meantime!

I had received an invitation to come down to the school and talk to the kids. Figured it was good diplomacy. Canadians think Americans won't do anything without getting paid and I wanted to show them that wasn't true. I got on my leggins, groomed the stock and off we went. While I was telling my story, most of the kids were spellbound. All except one little boy. He never said a word, just kept staring at my feet. Had his mouth open and started backing up. A teacher asked him, "Jimmy, what's wrong?"

"He's not a cowboy," the kid replied. "He's got on tennis shoes!"

Bears,
Moose
'n Flying Ticks

Heading towards Pochhontas, Alberta we passed several snowslides where snow had cascaded over the road. The rangers told us they had lost moose and big horn sheep in the slides. Everywhere you looked it was snow, snow, snow. We saw one area where a slide had wiped out a huge section of trees. Looked as though a giant lawnmower had ripped through the forest. In other places there was lodgepole pine so thick you couldn't even walk through it.

"It's weird the way the timberline goes through here," I said. "The trees grow up to 7,000 feet, then it's like somebody laid a ruler down on the mountain and chopped off all the greenery above."

"Sure thing, Tom. Dang trees go up to 'bout 11,000 down south."

Here in the glacier ice fields the snow was the reason for the trees not growing higher. Snow was 60 to 70 feet deep in some places! It lay in banks and never melted. There were places where it was broken off so we could see the thickness of it. We were in the heart of some of North America's most rugged country now.

141

"Boy, my face sure is snowburned."

"Yeah and my eyes sting. The glare off the bright snow is hell," answered Luke. We were squinting off to the west when I spied an unusual sight.

"Holy smoke, look at that moose!" I exclaimed. He was the most majestic animal I'd ever seen. And close too. I slipped off my horse to take a picture, but my dern camera had run to the end of the roll. While I was re-loading, a tourist saw us stopped on the side of the road and slammed on his brakes to see what we were doing. Of course, the noise scared the moose and he headed up into the timber.

"Oh, hell!" I said, "Wish people weren't so damn noisy."

A little later we saw a herd of rams. "Damn things act like they never seen a horse before," said Luke. Sure enough they ambled right on up to us. You'd have thought the scent of man would have scared them off. What a hunters paradise! But we had no lack of food now, so I wasn't about to shoot one. They were beautiful animals. A ram is a sheep with a full curl or better. Must of been 15 or 20 of them.

Part of a large herd of Big Horn Sheep in Jasper National Park, Alberta, Canada.

While we were sitting around the campfire that night Luke and I got to chawing about ideas for working up a new pack saddle. "We get home, I'm gonna get me some aluminum and make a new pack saddle. Change the design on it. With what I've found out packin' these last months, sure as hell oughta be able to build one you could pack seven days a week, 12 hours a day . . . and not worry about making your horse sore."

"Good idea, Tom. These packs sure ain't lasting. Making the stock sore too."

"Think those medicated sheep wool pads I bought the other day will work real good. Should be bettern' the ones made of foam rubber that I started out with. They wore out."

"I don't like them much anyway. They sweat and stay wet. Hard to get dry. They seem to scald the stock."

"If I had my druthers, it'd be a medicated sheep wool pad next to the animal's back, then a deer hair pad on top of that, then a foam rubber pad. Then if you use a wrap-around cotton blanket to go way down on their sides, like we're doin' now to keep the cinch from rubbin' them sore, it works out real good."

All of a sudden, a guy and a girl came loping into camp. He spoke like a machine gun in a high, excited voice. The guy, who claimed he was a photographer from Florida, said he'd had a nightmare about being confronted by bears. They were chasing him while he was furiously paddling a canoe.

"Four guys were crammed into one car with all their stuff," he told us. "They had the wing windows open for ventilation. And I had a bear next to my car window. Saw it with the light from my flashlight."

But when he woke up, their camper was actually *rocking*! "Threw me right out of bed," he said. "Bear stood up outside and he was taller than our truck. It was a nightmare in real life! It was a black bear. He finally went away," the man continued, exhausted.

"If it would've been a grizzly, it would've come right through the window if it took a mind," I told him.

"Oh, my God," murmured the woman.

"I've been watchin' out for bear. They'd rather have mule than anything else," I told them.

"Really? Black bear? They eat mules?"

"Black bear is all we have in Colorado," I said. "That's the reason we haven't got the seals on our rifles. Bear'll take a mule over a horse anytime."

"Horses' harder to catch," added Luke. "A mule, once they grab ahold 'o him, why they got him."

"Mule's better'n a watch dog" I said. "They'll let you know a bear's around before a dog will. You can be riding down the road and you can tell by your mule's ears when there's a bear around. If the wind is right, their ears'll perk up and they'll go to snortin'. Elk and moose don't bother them."

By this time the couple were more relaxed. We invited them to have a cup of coffee. Chatted about seeing signs of wolves, but none of the animals themselves. Then they gingerly picked their way back to their camper to spend the rest of the night.

The next evening, we had a visit from a park ranger. "Wouldn't put my sleeping bag under those trees there if I was you," he said.

"Why's that?"

"Flyin' ticks. Got 'em real bad up here. They'll jump on you by the hundreds. Half the people in this country is afraid to go out in the forest." He carried on about wood ticks being in the trees and kept warning us so, you'd have though the dern ticks were going to jump on you and eat you alive! He just couldn't believe that we would sleep right on the ground.

"Why, hell, we've been hanging 'round in these trees . . . ridin' under them, cuttin' them down, sittin' under them. Everything," I told him.

"Cripe, we ain't found no ticks on us," Luke told him. "'Course maybe we stink so bad, tick's couldn't get close to us."

The ranger failed to see the humor in Luke's remark. He stomped off shaking his head as though we were a couple of hopeless idiots.

Here Comes
The Ole Humane
Society

It was in Hinton that I had my major problem with the Humane Society. They had been trying on and off to shut me down, but they came the closest ever here. The paint mare, Joanne, had a sore on her back where she had rolled over by a stump and it had jabbed in her back. I'd been doctoring it and it was healing. They saw it under the saddle and thought that was terrible. Then they decided the stock was too lean. "Why, you aren't feeding and caring for these animals properly the way they look," the main man told me.

I came back with, "Did you ever see Mark Spitz when he was fat? Any person or animal in excellent physical condition is going to be lean."

Of course, Joanne being pregnant was another problem. She had been with me for almost 2,000 miles and now had come the time to part company. It was obvious she would be a mama in a very short time as her bag had already dropped. I wished I could stay around and see her new foal. But that wasn't possible. So I reluctantly traded her for a big buckskin gelding. "Buck"—as I decided to call him—had a habit of flipping over backwards on people. It was a nasty habit I intended to break him of.

We pulled into Hinton on my birthday, May 15th, and the

Elks had arranged a dance in my honor. It was a blast. Even collected 90 dollars in loot. Met a gal by the name of Sally who declared she "just had to ride with me a spell." She was six feet of dynamite. A red-headed, good looking woman if ever I saw one!

I ended up kicking around Hinton while the Humane Society deliberated on what to do about the animals. During that time I met an old outfitter who thought he had all the answers. Told me the boxes were too long and too heavy. Canadians don't pack but 100 to 125 pounds on their horses. Their pack saddles look like a jointed decker. The complainer told me the stock looked too thin . . . then turned around and told me not to bother packing grain. I told him to stick it where the sun don't shine!

He thought he was big time. Ran a pack train of 15 or 20 horses during one summer. 'Course his horses' total packing time was a week to 10 days and about 20 miles. And it would take them two days to cover the 20 miles! Then they'd come out, pick up a fresh string of horses, and take a new crop of people into the hills. No wonder his stock was fat, they didn't cover 2,000 miles! He was a loudmouth, bully type of guy that I got away from before I was tempted to punch out his lights.

After a week had passed, the same vet who had checked me across the border came up. He looked at the stock and gave us permission to go. "I'll deal with the Humane Society later," he said, waving us on.

About a half hour on the trail Buck decided to try his routine of flipping over backwards. Once was enough for me. The next time he reared up like he was going over backwards, I just stepped off and pulled him on over. When he hit the ground I administered a swift kick. After three more tries, he decided it made more sense for him not to do that anymore. It had taken six years for him to be broken of the habit!

Sally arrived as we were about five miles out of town. We had just crossed the Athabasca River, one of Canada's major waterways. She had a pickup with a couple of young horses in a stock rack in the back. Her boyfriend came with the horses, it seemed. As she mounted up he glared at me, told her not to be long, slammed the truck into reverse, and drove back towards town. I found it very hard to say to anyone who asked if they could come along, "No, you can't ride with me." It would really deflate their hopes. I had devised a way to let them come along for a bit, then decide to leave of their own accord. It was a simple plan. I just put in an extra long day! They soon felt the journey too stiff and bailed out. And not only did *they* get worn out, their stock quickly start lagging. So while I generally knocked off at four or five, Sally and I rode until eight o'clock that night.

It was a bad night, raining and the stock was restless. I soon discovered why. I could hear grizzly stalking the camp. I'd lay down and try to doze and as soon as the fire would begin to die down the animals would get restless. I'd have to get some more dry branches and wood to stoke it. The stock hugged the fire all night.

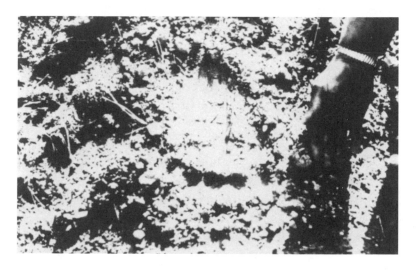

Mammoth grizzly tracks made my days and nights uneasy.

The next morning you could see where camp was by the smoke hanging in the air. I walked about 50 feet away and saw there was a trail worn where the grizzly had been circling the perimeter of camp. His paw mark was a big as both my hands

147

together! We were lucky I'd been too scared to sleep. He was out there waiting for the fire to die out so he could come into camp and eat.

The next day we made it into Grande Cash. Sally's boyfriend was there and packed her and the horses up and headed for home. She seemed downright glad to leave. Grande Cash is a little bitty logging and mining community. It has a dirt road and a forestry truck road. I was here because they had a TV station and the nearby exalted ruler of the Elks, the Chamber of Commerce and the TV representatives had just about hogtied me. People wouldn't let me just go make a camp and get some rest anymore. They had to hear all about our adventures. It was three A.M. before I got away from the TV studio. We taped an hour program, then shot the bull.

I'd left my stock at a trading post back on the main road, so they dropped me there. In Canada most trading posts are basically one room shacks with trapper's supplies. It's often snowy and muddy outside, so everybody pulls their boots off before going in. When I went into their little restaurant for coffee the next morning, there must have been 20 people inside. And there were 20 pair of shoes sitting just inside the door.

"Think we *finally* left the snow behind," I said to Luke as we rode along north of Grande Cash.

"Yup. Now the damn bugs'll start," came his cheering reply.

"You're right-on there. Saw a few mosquitos last night already. Man, look at these trees! Just like a wall-to-wall carpet of green. Sure is pretty."

That night we camped back off the road by a little creek. A fella and his wife, whom we had met in Grande Cash, came out with steaks for barbequing. They parked their pickup with a camper shell on the side of the road. While we were eating we started hearing something rattling around in the back of the pickup.

"Oh, God, I think I left the back door open!" said the man as he ran a little closer to check things out. We all hurried over and could see a little black bear that had crawled in through the open door of the camper. He was ransacking the place for a fare-thee-well.

"Start yelling and clapping your hands," I instructed. A chorus of shouts went up . . . and the bear made a hasty retreat.

"How'd you know what to do?" asked Luke.

"Black bears are afraid of humans," I replied. "Wish I could say the same for grizzlies!"

It was 26 degrees the next morning. There had been ice that night and a bit of rain, but the bugs seemed almost immune to the cold. By mid afternoon we had mosquitos, black deer flies, bullhead flies, greenhead flies and damn little buffalo gnats that the Indians call "no-see-ums" because the pesky things are so tiny. We hadn't expected to have bug problems yet, so had no repellent. "When we get into Grand Prairie the first place I'm headin' is for bug spray!" I said.

About an hour later here came three charter buses. They pulled along side of us and everybody gawked.

"Looks like a bunch of gophers in there," laughed Luke.

"Just hope they stay there. I thought for a minute back there the drivers were gonna stop and let everybody out. They'd flock us like a lynchin' mob! I was 'bout ready to take off!'"

"Hell, the way they all piled on the one side of the bus, they damn near tipped the thing over trying to get to the window to take pictures. Ain't it great to be popular?"

A few miles further I discovered I was popular in another way. Suddenly my beard started itching like crazy. I scratched at it and came up with a tick! Then a swarm of bugs hit me. As I brushed them from my face, off flipped another tick. "Hell, now I know what that ranger back there was talkin' about!" I said, "I feel like those little S.O.B.'s are crawling all over me!"

"Have to get you one of them collars like they put on dogs to keep the ticks off," chided Luke.

"Don't be so damn smart, buddy. If I got 'em—chances are you do too!" Luke didn't have anything to say after that, but I noticed he seemed to be digging at himself too.

In Grande Prairie we headed for a feed store, explained our trouble and found some bug repellent that the store owner said was sure to work. Was even supposed to discourage ticks! As we were leaving, another guy who had overheard our conversation tapped me on the shoulder.

"Howdy, cowboys, name's Crow. I'm with Forest Industries. I got somethin' I think you boys can really use, travelin' like you're doin' an' all."

With that he told us about having quantities of DMSO, which is a good medication for arthritis, sore muscles and saddle sores. I knew it to be a cure-all. You rub it on externally and within 10 minutes you can taste the damn stuff. *Real* potent! In the states it had cost me something like $30 for a half pint. In Grande Prairie I bought a 55-gallon drum of the stuff. Had it shipped down on logging trucks and spent $110 altogether. Figured when I got back home I'd cut it with 1/3 alcohol and sell it for a fortune!

After making such a deal, it seemed only fair to do something nice in return. So we visited a reform school that had kids 15 to 18 and gave them a talk. They seemed real glad to see some new faces and hear what it was like in America and on the road.

Grande Prairie is known for the great white whooping crane. We went through the museum and bird sanctuary. The cranes are nearly extinct, only 1,000 strong now. They hatch right in that area. Make their nests near town on a migrating waterfowl flyway. Like the cranes, we were anxious to be on our way to the next stop.

"How Do You Do," Miss Dominion of Canada!

The first day out of Grande Prairie we were riding along when a guy came up and offered us a beer. We reined in and chatted with him a bit and were sipping on the beer when along came another car and pulled up. He called the other man by name and shouted, "Go on now, Bill, and don't delay these cowboys. They need to be on their way and get into town." I was tired, enjoying the beer and the man's company, and had no intention of hurrying into town. I told the intruder that in just so many words. He seemed a bit surprised, but turned around and headed back where he had come from without anymore said.

Eventually, we finished up and headed on towards Beaverlodge. Pretty soon here comes this brand new cadillac with three pretty girls in it. And it slowed down. "Things is looking up," commented Luke.

When the car stopped, the girls, clad in only bikinis, climbed out and came over and introduced themselves. It turned out to be Miss Dominion of Canada and her two runners-up! That was like meeting Miss America! She explained that they had made arrangements for her to officially meet us in Beaverlodge where they were having a big annual fund-raising dinner that night, that was why they wanted us to hurry. After

151

we assured the girls we would proceed with haste, they climbed back into the cadillac with their chaperone and disappeared.

"Hot damn!" shouted Luke. "Of all the luck! You better believe we'll be there fast!"

"Man, those honeys must have been freezin' in those skimpy bikinis. Here it is spittin' rain and I've got on a down coat!"

"Don't mind lookin' at their goose bumps none," Luke said with a sneer. "You better believe we'll hussle right on into town."

When we rode into Beaverlodge there were about 15 cars and 60 or so people gathered to greet us. Not bad for a little town of 1500. The mayor was there and a reporter from the local paper. We were made honorary members of their travel bureau.

At the fund-raising dinner we were seated at the head table with four famous hockey stars from throughout Alberta. We were introduced as honored guests and mentioned in several of the talks. After dinner they put us up in a hotel that proclaimed "welcome" on its marquee and made us feel very much at home.

I danced 'til nearly daylight. Miss Dominion was a real pretty girl and very intelligent. She was a little overly refined for me. Everything had to be done with just the right etiquette and this and that. I guess that can be expected from someone in her position. Figured I wouldn't ever meet anybody else like that. It was quite an evening.

Since it was about time to trade off the bay, I sought out a source for fresh stock. Made a deal for a big black sonofagun that looked like he would make a sturdy mount. We'd have to go out about four miles to pick him up, but figured he was worth it. Then an old horse trader name of Jonas heard I was looking and tried to sell me a horse. I refused since I was satisfied with the black gelding. Jonas said, "Well, Tom, since you've got the deal made, I'll just go pick him up for you. That way you won't have to ride out of you way."

So we started on our way and kept waiting for Jonas to show up. Ten miles later he still hadn't arrived with the horse. "He's an old geiser—must be close to 90—suppose he had a heart attack or something?" asked Luke.

Before I could answer, here comes Jonas pulling a horse trailer. He gets a quarter mile ahead of us, backs up to a slight incline and starts to unload the horse.

"That's not my horse!" I told him. Then he comes on with this tale that when he was loading the black horse, it reared up and went over backwards and broke its neck. And he knew I just had to have another horse, so he brought me this one of his. It was a big, flabby, listless horse that I disliked from the moment I saw it. It was a horse that would hold you back, not fit to be in the string; a horse that would mean trouble.

Ridin'
The Alcan Highway

We put up that night at a little place called Demmit. It consisted of a gas station and grocery store arrangement. The new horse was proving as disappointing as I had expected. He was lazy and especially thin-skinned. The bugs bothered him even worse then the other stock.

"Just think Luke, we're almost to the Alcan Highway. From there it'll be downhill all the way. Only 1,250 miles to go. We've almost got it whipped!"

"Just where's the Alcan start?" Luke asked.

"At Dawson Creek. The first 10 miles are blacktop . . . then it's a dirt road from then on."

We hit Dawson Creek and crossed back into British Columbia on June first. It was a welcome 50 degrees. "We've got that green grass and clear sailin' for sure!" I told Luke.

There were mile markers alongside the road so you could gauge how far you'd gone. At first it stretched ahead of us as straight as sighting down a gun barrel. Later the road made a big, sweeping curve that appeared to waste a lot of time. I decided we'd just take a shortcut and go straight across. It was then I discovered that the engineers who built the Alcan Highway were no dummies. My shortcut was full of muscag. A real bog! When the horses walked across it, the whole ground shook.

155

It's all water underneath, with six to 18 inches of peatmoss over the top. If you punch a hole in it the water bubbles up and immediately fills the hole. Now it is true that a horse or mule can walk across it . . . if they don't step in a previous footprint. If they walk where an animal has just trod, however, they'll sink to their knees in the mush. This lesson I learned first hand.

The soggy tundra is almost like quicksand.

Further along we came across the river that feeds Charlie Lake. It was about 100 yards wide. "No problem. There's a bridge across it," pointed out Luke. Well, bridges in the northern country are built so that in the winter the snow and ice doesn't build up on them. They're almost like our cattle guards—railroad irons laid across so the snow will filter through. Some even have 2" by 2" steel mesh with jagged edges to keep it from getting slick. The stock balked at walking on the lattice-work bridge. "Dern things are afraid they'll get stuck. They just flat won't cross." I said in frustration.

"Ya suppose if we waited awhile somebody'd come along with a horse trailer?" asked Luke.

"Not likely. Indians are the main horse owners in Canada

and they don't haul them."

"Come to think of it, we ain't seen a horse trailer in some time."

"Seems we've got just one choice. Looks like we're gonna get wet." First I unsaddled all but my horse and put the saddles and gear by the bridge. Then I led the stock out into the river. It was a gentle flow and they did pretty well. After I got my mount across I had the joyful job of going back and carrying all the saddles and gear across the damn bridge. By then we had attracted quite an audience. They were taking bets on whether or not we would be successful. Fortunately, a couple of them volunteered to help lug some stuff across. After I got everything resaddled and reloaded on the other side I was ready to collapse!

After crossing the river, we could see it was starting to be tundra, flat peatmoss prairie. It stretched out for several miles. We were out on it about a quarter of a mile when Trashy quit me. She started falling in, so she just laid down and wouldn't budge an inch!

"Damn mules," I exclaimed. "They won't do a thing if they think it'll hurt 'em, you know. You hit boggy ground and they'll just lay down on ya and wait until somebody takes off their pack and makes it safer and easier. Not like a horse. It'll hurt itself tryin' to please its owner."

"Not no mule. Now I know where they got that there saying about mules: speak softly and carry a big stick. What we gonna do?"

"Have to double back over with Mula and the big bay horse. Tie 'em to a tree and use their weight to skid her out. While I get them ready, you get her unsaddled and unpacked." I went over and rolled her and tied a rope around her belly. Then the other mule and horse proceeded to skid her along like a fat log coming out of the forest.

As soon as Trashy got to solid ground she started thrashing to get up, so I stopped and let her regain her footing and walk out. The ordeal of sliding on the grass had burned her withers and the top of her hips. She looked kinda weird, like a bald eagle with her hair sliced clear off.

157

Just to be different, Trashy is acting balky.

At Fort St. John we met an old timer who told us how to keep down the problem with the flies and bugs. They were so bad you needed a flame thrower to repel 'em! This old codger recommended mudding the horses and mules. Said the black mud or creek mud would keep mosquitoes off real good. The mud also helped camouflage the burn marks on Trashy.

It was here that we encountered half-inch-long horseflies. They were called greenhead flies and they were so bad I had to wear my rain slicker for protection. They went right through my heavy denim shirt and long johns. The damn things would get on the horses between their front legs and in their groin area where the horses couldn't reach them and bite up a storm. They have a set of pinchers. When they bite, the blood just keeps running. I got ahold of some old Army blankets and opened them up under the saddles to flop and help scare away the dirty devils.

Made another good connection at Fort St. John. I met a man from the Canadian Freight Lines and he sold me enough oats— 1,200 pounds—to take us to Fairbanks. The deal was that Loiselle Trucking and White Pass Trucking would help shuffle the feed for me. They agreed to drop it off at trading posts along the Alcan as close to 100 miles apart as they could get. There had been publicity ahead, so the people at the posts were cooperative. I met the dispatcher in the Elks Lodge and he did all the scheduling . . . didn't even have to pay any freight or service charge; just paid for the oats themselves. That finally took the $100 emergency mad money I'd been given at the start, plus all my gambling winnings. But I felt good about it as it meant the stock had oats for the rest of the trip, yet it lessened the load they would have to carry.

I also ran into a man named Mr. Keen. We met through his employee, Bob Kennedy. Keen had racehorses and helped me shop around for fresh stock. We didn't find any suitable animals that I could afford, but he did put me up in a hotel and let the stock stay at his ranch.

I thought it strange I heard a gal was in town trying to buy horses too. Supposedly she was riding from El Paso to Fairbanks and needed a fresh mount. That story really caught my interest! The guys who told me about her directed me to a nearby bar. Sure enough she was siddled up to the bar bragging and letting guys buy her drinks as she told the story of her trip. She was a big, old, burly-looking woman. When I walked up she was relating how one of her horses had run off and she had broke a leg on another. "Been a long, hard trip from El Paso," she boasted.

"That's interesting," I said. "I come from El Paso and I'll be damned if I've seen you anywhere along the trail!"

With that her eyes widened, she murmured something about the ladies room and slipped off the stool, quickly disappearing to the back of the bar.

I was hopping mad! Here was this phoney sopping up all the attention. And I was so damn flat broke I didn't even have a buck to buy a beer with.

"Guess you showed her," said a satiny-smooth voice. I turned to see a wiry, well-built woman who looked to be in her early twenties. "I'm Ginny," she said with a slow smile. As it turned out Ginny was a hustler who had been working up in Alaska for the last three years. She had known a lot of the guys on the pipeline. Now she was hooking down in Fort Nelson at a big oil field going in there. "I'm on my way home to Albuquer-

159

que next month," she told me. "I've saved all my money and now I can buy me a little house and meet a nice guy and settle down." Ginny bought me two rounds of drinks and sat fascinated as I told her the details of my story. She ended up also buying me a couple pairs of levis, a new shirt and a brand new pair of boots before I left.

I Take
a Shine to a Lady

Traveling along the highway a couple of days later I came upon an unusual sight. There in the middle of the road was a big, stranded Winnebago motor home. In front of it, strewn out on a bedsheet spread in the road, were all the transmission parts. I rode up and started talking.

It seemed the Reisler party was from Tucson and their 26-foot Winnebago had broken down here in the middle of nowhere. While the father of the family normally earned his living as a photographer, the situation had forced him to play amateur auto mechanic. There were no service stations anywhere around.

"We've got that toyota over there," said a friendly young woman. "We use it to drive into Fort Nelson for parts." I soon learned the family consisted of parents, grandparents, a brother and the girl—Trixy—who was a real doll in a sort of hippy way. She looked to be in her early twenties and had thick brown hair clear down to her belt. It appeared to be in everyone's best interest that I lend a hand with the repair job.

The next day Trixy rode with me using my extra horse, as Luke had disappeared again. We were headed around Muncho Lake. It was a peaceful ride and we were enjoying the scenery and getting better acquainted when along came a trailer cavalcade. Must have been 200 Airstream travel trailers pass us, bumper-to-bumper! They stirred up enough dust to choke 50 horses! When Trixy's folks caught up with us that night everything seemed to be going fine with the Winnebago. I camped near by their motor home and Trixy gathered up some gear and waved goodbye to her family again the next morning. They were driving on ahead and we were to meet them further along the highway.

Later that day we came by some hot springs and decided to go in swimming. They were little gravel-bottomed pools with water about 80 degrees. After sitting in the pool for a half hour I was so damn weak I couldn't do anything! That mineral water really sucks it out of you.

Trixy was quite a gal. One of the nicest, classiest people I've ever known. I found out she was 22, had been married, but was divorced now. She was a person you'd be proud to take around and show off. She seemed to feel the same way about me.

We were at 1,200 feet elevation where you could sit up and watch the sun go around in a circle. It never set and the moon never really came up. It was like somebody just adjusted a giant dimmer switch. You could still see the glow when the sun actually came up at three A.M. It was so strange the way the sun shone high at midnight and you could see both the moon and the sun at the same time. It made Trixy's face kind of flushed. She got a real buzz out of it and so did I.

The next morning we stayed in the sack until about 8:30. We were in no big hurry, so we ate a leisurely breakfast and got moving by 10. Rode past a big fat black bear. We were able to get the horses within 60 feet of him. Then they started getting snorty. Can't say I blame them. He was about 400 pounds and looked to be a three-year-old.

A bit further we came upon some construction work going on. There were two guys on jack hammers and the stock got spooky when we were still quite far away. I dismounted and went up to see what we could do. They were real helpful in shutting down their jackhammers for us to go by. Luke was waiting up the road a spell, looking worse for his sidetrip. That evening we caught up with the Winnebago again and Trixy re-joined her family.

Going toward Fort Nelson it was pretty routine riding. Trashy had started to develop a fistulous, which is a swelling in the withers. It's usually caused from a bruise the animal gets from rolling on a rock or stick. The bruised muscle over the bone gets a puss pocket under it like a boil. Trashy's had gotten almost the size of a football, so I decided to trade her off. Found a stout, good-looking horse and said goodbye to the mule.

Fate didn't intend for Trashy and me to part company, however. Half a day down the trail the new horse I'd just traded for came up lame. He had a bad knee that didn't show up until he was ridden a bit. So we turned around and headed back as I knew I could doctor Trashy and have a better animal than a lame horse that wasn't going to get any better. That night we lanced the sore and drained it. Then I made a mud pack of the black river mud and moss and put it on the sore spot. "It'll draw out the poison and keep the flies off," I told Luke. I cut a hole in the saddle pad so it would fit around the pack and lightened her load, so Trashy was in pretty good shape by the time we hit the road again.

The biggest problem was the bugs. It got so we'd take off in the daytime and ride at night. There wasn't such a bug population at night. And it was light enough to read a newspaper at midnight, so seeing wasn't any problem. I wasn't affected by the day/night reversal in riding as I slept a lot in the saddle. In the day time we'd pull off, mud the stock so they wouldn't be pestered so by insects and let them take it easy.

Another good thing about riding at night was I didn't have so many tourists stopping me. This was a relief. Each time somebody stopped us it meant a delay of a half hour or so by the time they heard about the trip, took pictures, got autographs and such. To top things off, Luke and I had a big falling out and I ran him out of camp.

I was beginning to be concerned about getting back home in time. The Stampede in Monte Vista was the end of July and I was working the stock hard to make up some lost time.

In addition to bugs, time, and Luke pushing me, crossing the rivers was becoming a big hassle. It was not only a lot of work to unsaddle and unpack the stock, get them across then re-do everything, there was the problem of getting *me* across. My mama used to tell me she thought I was part cat the way I hated water. From necessity, I had learned a few basic swimming strokes, but I disliked the water and was a mediocre swimmer at best. When we came to the East River it was deeper and swifter than any we had forded before. You better believe I heaved a big sigh of relief when the stock and I were safely across! I was to find out before long that the challenge of river crossings had just begun!

This was the heart of grizzly country now. Saw a lot of tracks and the horses were nervous. I wasn't nervous . . . I was plain scared! I didn't want to lose any stock, let alone myself! Saw several timber wolves. They run in families but you mainly see one at a time. They stuck pretty close to me. When I'd make camp I'd build a fire, make supper, then play the harmonica. Course it was never really dark, so that helped. And my harmonica playing kept everything out of camp.

Game was abundant. There were lots of moose; nearly all had twins and a lot of triplets. I was excited when I saw my first dahl sheep. They're the same as big horn sheep, only white. Also saw big herds of caribou, up to 200 animals at once. I always thought a caribou was a caribou, but around there I was told they had plains caribou and tree caribou.

The fishing was great! I caught a lake trout must have weighed 25 pounds. The big sucker was almost three feet long. Filleted it, ate some, then carried the rest of the cooked flesh in my saddle bags.

Had real good luck catching pike too. I discovered that the lakes right on the Alcan highway are hopeless for fishing though. Within a half mile of the road they're all dead. When the U.S. Army engineers completed the highway, the trucks, cats and machinery they were finished with, they just drove out and parked on the frozen lakes along the highway! In the spring when the thaw came, all the equipment sank to the bottom. Eventually, as barrels and tanks rusted out, the spilled diesel fuel and grease killed off the fish and polluted the water. I thought the guy who told me this story was kidding, but I later learned this was actually the way they got rid of the equipment so they wouldn't have to haul it home.

I'd also heard that in the early seventies there was an outfit in eastern Canada that decided they were going to freight wagons west. They started out the first of April and hadn't gone 100 miles when a snowstorm struck. They got sick and didn't know how to camp or feed their horses. The wagons broke down and the horses weakened. They didn't even make 300 miles. Wrong stock. Nothing thought out. Poorly prepared. It was one of the biggest fiascos I'd heard of.

I wasn't about to make their mistake. Having a third of the trip left, probably posed two-thirds of the problems I'd face, especially with the stock looking tired and Luke and I not getting on too smooth. I knew I was defying the odds. Was I prepared to meet what was ahead?

The World's
Greatest
Gold Panner

"Mighty unusual. Most unusual year we've had in the 65 years I've been here." The words came from an old man of 81, named Jess Starnes. He might have been past 80, but he moved like a youngster. He was a world champion gold panner and consultant to the tourist association. "Ain't never had no winter. Very seldom I put on a jacket all winter long. Since we never had no winter, don't feel like spring or summer. In the early days we'd have 25, 26 inches of rainfall and that produced a good crop every year." I was sure glad to have missed out on the 26 inches of rain! It was see-your-breath weather now, crisp but reasonably nice.

As the old fella fiddled with his gear, he kept talking like a living history book. He proved that everybody is intelligent, just on different subjects. Pointing at my horses, he said, "Before there was horses come to this country, the Slavey Indians up north, their main asset was women. What they did—the Crees and the Beavers lived down here—the Slaveys would come down here every three or four years and would raid for pack dogs and all the young women they could gather up. They was better fighters and if they had to kill a few Crees and Beavers,

167

why they did. Then they'd disappear back in the country they call the Headless Valley. People would go in there and never come out. When somebody would find 'em, they'd find a skeleton with no head on it."

He told of his people leaving Cleveland, Texas in a covered wagon in 1898, going first to Oklahoma, then to Southern Alberta, "Homesteaded out on the bald prairie where there wasn't nothing bigger than a rose bush. In them days the wind was wicked. When we came was only 30 or 40 white people living in the whole area. The postmaster helped me reserve a piece of land 'til I could file a claim on it at 18."

Jess and his people didn't have any money. They lived off the land. "Been doin' it ever since," he said. "For 40 years I ran a trapline. Then in the thirties, I started dabbling around when I could get $36 an ounce for gold. The Peace River had fine gold where you shovel about 50 ton of rock and gravel into a sluice box to get an ounce. Nobody works that way no more when you get $40 or $50 a day for common labor."

He invited me inside his place and showed me a big container full of black gravel. Then he took out a little bottle with a half-inch of gold flakes at the bottom. Poured the bottle over the gravel and mixed it all together. Started panning. Talked as he worked and every once in a while picked out a flake of gold with a pair of tweezers. He was fast and sure of himself. We talked about game and natural kill cycles. "Ain't no cycle on the wolves," he explained. "They're big animals and they eat a lot of wild meat. Wherever there's game in this north country, you'll find wolves.

"With rabbits, in the early days it was a seven-year cycle. And the native people followed a seven-year cycle with their trapping expeditions. One year after all the rabbits died off, the coyotes, foxes and the like was much easier to trap 'cause their feed was scarce." All the while he's talking, he's panning, panning.

"Beaver's a 35-year cycle. For a long time there was no beaver. It was the end of the cycle. Then there was beaver all over. Two things helped. During the last big war people could make money easier than trapping. And nowadays the price of beaver fur isn't high enough. Every creek and pond in this country has got beaver in it. He went on to tell me how beaver prefer little trees like willows and poplar. "I know a dam that's 35 feet high and 15 miles long," he continued. "Beavers built it and a huge lake. Up north they had overrun the streams in the area, so they went on a water slope and built a wing dam to catch the runoff and make their own lake where there was no running stream at all! Beaver's quite an animal all the way around." He told of being crippled in the war and becoming a processor, buying from trappers and getting on the average $80 for a good beaver. One year the high was $48 at auction, compared to $10 in the early days.

I was really warming up to the old guy and enjoying his company. "What do you think of Big Foot?" I asked him.

"That's a hoax. The museum in Alpine, Texas they got artifacts that are like Indian things. Flat tools and things big in proportion. So I figure there was a race of big people, but they disappeared completely without any explanation.

"Then folks began seein' strange things. The sasquatch in British Columbia is a grizzly bear in the spring of the year that's half shed off. Like a big cinnamon bear, he'll shed and get pale in color. He's ragged and big and you see an animal like that in the bush and he looks altogether different than the normal slick bear that's shed off. People see them things and report 'em as big foot. I've seen grizzly tracks supposedly look like a person's foot . . . they're nine inches wide and got claws on 'em. Wanna hear a funny story?"

"Sure thing," I replied.

"The road department wanted to build a road through an Indian reservation just west of Calgary in the foothills. The natives, it was their land; they'd lived there 10,000 years and didn't want no road and people running all over where they fished and hunted. So they dressed up a man that was seven feet tall in a bearskin and made big tracks. They scared the road surveyors near out of their skins! The road department never did build that road. The Indians laugh about it yet." I understood just how they felt. And I had to chuckle at the ingenious way they solved their problem.

"Grizzly, when they come out of their dens in the spring, they're meat hungry," Jess explained. "Fact is, they'll eat anything. To a grizzly it don't make a speck of difference if it's a horse or a moose." He told about camping on the muskeg with a bunch of huskies. "There was a terrific commotion about two o'clock in the morning. We got up and the dogs were raising hell and the horses were excited. It wasn't quite light enough to tell a bear from a horse. Fella with me grabbed his gun and ran right out into the middle of 'em. I couldn't shoot nothing because he was there and the horses were milling around. We were lucky. It was an old female with two yearlings, last year's cubs. He ran right into that confounded female. Knew what he was doin' and he killed her dead. The dogs chased the cubs out. He didn't lose a horse, but three dogs bit the dust."

All the while he had been talking he was sifting through the gravel. "What about gold pannin', can you really make a living at it?" I asked.

He said you might do okay, but you'd have to have enough to live on for two or three years until you found the right place to do it. Buying equipment was too expensive; he recommended finding a natural fine gold bar and shoveling rock to find the gold. "Bought this here gold pan at Edmonton in 1913," he said. "You can wash dishes in it, bake bread in it, render lard in it, do most anything. But if you got grease in it, before you pan gold you better burn it off. You can't get no fine gold with a greasy pan."

He went on to say he washed gold in the river from 1930 to '34. Five years ago he did it again for the "Pan-a-thon" where people sponsored panners for so much a ton. He went into the world championships with that. "Got a phone call yesterday," he related. "The British Columbia government wants to pay to send me down to Atlanta, Georgia for three days to demonstrate how to pan for gold. Got no objections. I been doin' it free up to now."

Jess Starnes might have been 81 years old, but the years rolled away as he held that big old pan and searched the bits of gravel for the gold he knew was there. And when he was finished, the little bottle held exactly the same amount of gold flakes it had when he started. I knew when I left I'd been privileged to see a champ.

Moldy Rolls
and Skeeters

By mile marker 135 we ran across an old boy who had a deal set up to feed the bears. He brought us out some bear food too. Guess we looked 'bout as ratty as the bears. My beard was really dirty. I hadn't had a chance to wash it lately real good and the dirt was about to drive me crazy. It was itching and dusty. This dirt road was miserable! There were all sorts of vehicles on the Alcan—from cars piled high with sleeping bags and tents to fancy trailers and motor homes to commercial rigs to passenger cars. But they all had one thing in common: every damn one of them stirred up a ton of dust!

The fella's "bear food" consisted of four-day-old cinnamon rolls, bread and fruitcake. "May be moldy," he told us, "But just break the mold off and you're dang sure welcome to it. Be sure to keep your guns handy and loaded though, the bears they're used to me feedin' 'em 'round here." We didn't need further encouragement to be cautious.

"One thing for sure," I told Luke. "This goldang stuff feels fresher than some of the junk we been buyin'!"

The bear feeder went on to tell us to be on the lookout for caribou tracks. "Leave a track like a full grown moose, except they're more pointed, like a deer print. And on the back of the track, there's dew claws touching the ground and poking two little holes. Damn near looks like they got four toes instead of two."

"Sounds like B.S. to me," commented Luke when we got out of earshot. "Ain't no way in hell they can leave a track like that." We kept our eyes on the ground as well as looking around us to see if we could pick up any tracks. Sure enough a little while later we saw some on soft ground that looked just like the old fella had described. Also ran across a wolf claw nearly as big as my hand. It was four or five inches across. Looked like he'd been running along the road up and down looking for rabbits. Must of been a big bugger.

We had a comfortable camp that night. The bears and the bugs seemed to have business elsewhere, so we sat back enjoying the smell of the wood burning as the campfire danced, having a smoke and listening as a nearby creek bubbled over some rocks.

The next day we only made 23 miles. Problem was the feed that was supposed to be dropped off hadn't shown up. We met up with the trucker, but he didn't have it and said the load wouldn't be coming through until the following day. So he gave us a lift to an airport where outfitters fly in. There we traded for 100 pounds of grain. It was old crushed up crap that the horses wouldn't hardly even eat. After we got back on the road, a lady pulled up who had heard of our plight. She had 80 pounds of good oats. We tried to pay her, but she wouldn't take any money.

Thank goodness the horses had decent food, 'cause they were in misery otherwise. The mosquitoes and little black flies were eating them up! Their bellies and groins were covered with them. Their ears too. Poor ears were just bloody from the flies chewing on them. We tried fly dope but it didn't work very well and you can't hardly mud horses' ears!

We hit Fort Nelson June 16th. It was there I met a gentleman by the name of Robert Manji. Turned out he owned African Safaris in Kenya. "Seeing how you're an adventurous young man, I'd like to teach you how to hunt big game in Africa," he

174

told me. "I'll teach you . . . and if you like it and want to stay, I'll get you set up and get your guide license."

It was a very tempting proposition. But if I went, it had to be right then and I had to stay 90 days at least. He told me that a professional hunter with one client got paid $300 a day. And it ranged up to $800 a day if you took out four clients. "You'll hunt anything from giant gazelles to red bucks to wildebeasts," he continued.

"Sorry, Mr. Manji, but I've got too much tied up in this trip. I've come too far to give it up now," I told him, wondering as the words poured from my mouth if I was making one of the biggest mistakes of my life.

This French cavalry pack saddle will fit any horse.

We were riding through a beautiful area. Nature, in her great wisdom, weaves a tapestry of wonder. As we rode along I recognized wild roses, strawberries, garlic, onions and elderberries. Many of the threads that combined to make the colorful garment were unfamiliar to me. There appeared to be about 40 different kinds of flowers and plants.

"Wish the river weren't so dern muddy. I could sure go for some fish."

"Dig out some of that peanut butter and jelly we bought yesterday. Wish we had some milk, but at 95¢ a quart, that's almost $4 a gallon. Too rich for my blood."

"That guy back at the store said we'd be hitting even rougher road pretty soon didn't he?"

"Yeah. Just what we need. But at least it's gettin' shorter! This last leg'll be hell. Need shoes for Trashy and Mula and no way to get 'em. Need a day off for us too, but I don't see that either. Sure would be nice to rest up some instead of bustin' our asses all the time." My attitude wasn't too good that day. It was an uphill ride nearly the whole way. We climbed 1,500 feet over 32 miles. It was hard on the horses and hard on us. Time was a real bind.

"Think we're gonna have to go to ridin' 12 hours on, 12 hours off."

"How's that gonna work, Tom?"

"We'll get up about three, get saddled and packed and feed the stock. That'll take about two hours. Then we'll ride for 10 hours. About half-way during the ride, we'll stop and let 'em feed again. Since they'll be workin' extra hard, we'll give 'em plenty of grain." It was still a mighty stiff order. I wasn't sure either the stock—or the people—were up to it.

Eating dust on the Alcan Highway.

Befriended
by the Indians

The area north of Fort Nelson was populated mainly by Indians, which the tourists called Eskimos. They are a friendly sort of people. Luke had bailed again, so it was good to have some company. Had heard about me on the radio and stopped me to see if there was anything I needed and invited me to one of their villages. There were villages spotted along the highway every 25 or 30 miles.

A typical village consisted of one room hogans or wooden shacks made of one by sixes with no insulation, no paint and just a wood barrel stove in the middle. In the past, the government went in and built them modern homes to upgrade the quality of life. Then the Indians moved their horses, goats and sheep *into* the new homes. The government can't seem to understand that they are a proud people and want basically to be left alone to live like they have for centuries.

Horses run all over in the villages and everybody who is anybody has eight or 10 husky dogs. The huskies are used in the winter with sleds. They bark constantly, one causing a chain reaction to begin that makes more ruckas than a rock band with the best amplifiers. After the peace and quiet I'd gotten accustomed to, it really bothered me.

I got well acquainted with one Indian man named Marvin

Toogood. He was the younger brother of a chief and a real interesting person. He invited me to stay for dinner, which was caribou. Since they have no refrigeration and most live without electricity, their diet is mainly fish and canned caribou and moose. Marvin took me out the next day and showed me where to fish and how to smoke my catch quick to preserve them. While we were fishing, his wife made me a very welcome pair of mucklucks.

"Here something to cure your horses bites," Marvin told me. "It is made of different roots. Leave it until you ready to put it on. Then peel it off like a ratabega, mash into juice, mix together and rub on. Works good. Especially on bit 'em no-see-'em bugs." It was important that they had a good insect repellent. There are a lot of hunting camps in the area and the Indians rent their horses to the outfitters who cater to hunters from the lower 48. The Indians also use the horses to pack out their own game.

"What do you feed your stock?" I asked.

"Don't," replied Marvin. He explained that in the fall they turn everything loose to fend for itself. In the spring they round up what horses made it through the winter. It's cheaper to buy another horse than to feed all through the winter. What they lose they go to Edmonton or Calgary to replace.

I learned that about fifty percent of the Indians are winos. They have little purpose in life, so turn to drink. My friend warned me to watch my livestock and possessions as some of his people would take anything to buy booze with.

Moving on, I was wishing I had a couple of hundred dollars to buy another horse. The bay's withers had swelled up and he had two scald marks on him. The SPCA would have shut me down if they had caught me. Thank goodness the road had good shoulders. But there wasn't much grass; I was mighty dependent on the truckers grain drops.

It was lonesome country, didn't see many other folks to talk to. Did notice a snowshoe rabbit though. Going about four miles per hour I talked to the livestock and sometimes I talked to myself. Got to playing the mouth harp some and both mules started braying. When it's quiet, old cowboy music comes to you that you wouldn't think of otherwise.

June 25th I crossed the Yukon border and made it into Watson Lake. There was a real surprise waiting for me there. They have a signpost corner and there was a sign from Alamosa city limits! Made me feel almost homesick. Another surprise came when Luke hitchhiked in. It only took us a few hours, however, to have another fight and split up.

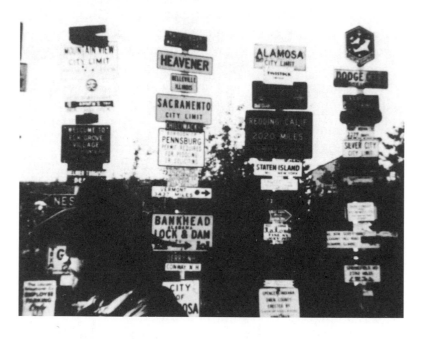

Sign post corner at Watson Lake in the Yukon.

Met a guy called Mark Barnes and he invited me out to his cabin to meet his wife and rest the stock a bit. "They call me a squatter," said Mark. "We came up here, set down our asses on this land and started building us a 60 x 50 log cabin. Still long way to finished, as you can see.

179

"And all our stuff's in that yonder 10 by 12 cabin. Not even room for a mouse in there," added his wife. "But we do okay. Got five goats, two horses, 34 chickens, three dogs and a goofy cat. We sell eggs and milk and that gives us money to buy coffee and flour and stuff like that. And Mark traps in the winter."

"Know any way I can pick up some bucks?" I asked.

"You any good at shoein' horses?" asked Mark.

"You bet! Been doin' it enough on this dang trip!"

"Then you're set. I know of five head a guy owns that need shoein' real bad. And there's probably more to be had. Ain't many farriers in these parts."

Over the next few days it seemed like I shoed every horse in existence! I also taught Mark a thing or two. He had killed a black bear the day before, a nice one with as good a hide as I'd ever seen. But he didn't know how to pelt it out and he didn't know how to take care of the meat. Some trapper.

When I got there he had it hanging in his well! Had the well all contaminated. Goldangest mess you ever saw with flies buzzing around and dead flies in the water. And he and his wife were drinking the water, even with blood dripping in it! "You'll be dead 'fore you know it, you keep drinkin' that contaminated water," I warned them. We tried to save the meat, but it had spoiled and we wound up throwing it away.

I decided since they'd had such bad luck with the bear that I'd give them a hand at getting their cabin more finished. They had the logs skidded up, but didn't have them peeled so I cut some 18 and 24 inch stumps and set them up as the foundation. "Let's get these logs peeled and notched, then we can set 'em up," I suggested. None of us had ever built a log cabin before so it was a blind-lead-the-blind proposition.

"How you suppose we gonna get them big logs on top?" Mark asked.

"It's about time these horses earned their keep. We'll build a big tripod thing over the center, then use our horses and hook up to the saddle horns and hoist up the logs."

The idea worked. Towards the end of the third day we had everything but the roof poles up. "You're gonna be on your own now, folks. I've gotta get on the road early tomorrow," I told them. "The stock is good and rested and my time's runnin' short."

Doin' laundry at Watson Lake in the Yukon.

"We sure appreciate your help, Tom. Say, let's get us in some good fishing this evening, so's you've got some to take with you." His cabin overlooked what he called "No-name-Lake." It had pike in it as long as your leg. The water was very clear and very cold—glacier water. There were minnows and fresh shrimp for the pike to eat, so they refused to bite. "You have to take your line and put a big spinner on it and hook 'em in the side or the tail and reel 'em in," Mark said. We literally "hooked" several with three-pronged snag hooks. Then we filleted them, ran a stick through them and hung them over an open fire. By cooking them real slow they made a kind of smoked jerky for the upcoming trip's groceries.

181

Grizzly on My Trail!

When I left Mark's place I decided to pull back off the road and quit riding the Alcan. The stock had enjoyed a good rest and were fresh, so I felt okay about riding them hard for awhile.

The Canadian borders have cut lines about 16 feet wide where they go through with a D9 cat and plow it out for a fire break. Most of them are set up in two mile squares. When you look down one it's cleared of timber as far as you can see. The line may go right straight up over a cliff. Nothing stops it. I figured that by following the cut lines I could omit about 75 miles of travel. But there were some other things I hadn't figured on!

A little while later a big grizzly hit the cutline and fell in behind me. When he first appeared, I thought the stock was going to run me over! They were so scared they tried to huddle around me. Couldn't say I blamed them. This old boar must have weighed almost 1,200 pounds. He was a fierce-looking gladiator. He plundered along on all fours and was as tall as Trashy. Had a stallion-like roach of hair, a long snout and a dished-in face. Because he was from the glacier country, his dark protective fur was so long it almost dragged the ground as he walked.

Right after the grizzly "joined our party" I took my shotgun, threw a slug in the barrel, and rode with it laying across my lap. He wandered along about 100 yards back and didn't do anything, but put a crink in my neck because I kept looking back wondering what he *might* do!

The old boar would get out from behind me and I thought maybe he was going to circle us. When he faded into the forest that way I'd get especially nervous. And the stock were pretty fidgety when they couldn't see him back there. They kept craning their necks to turn their heads back to watch him. Whenever he'd disappear, I knew he was getting closer just be the spooky way they acted. Then he'd reappear to loiter in back of us again, and the horses and mules would settle down some. But they still kept a wary eye on him.

I made camp along the border that night. The stock needed to rest. Of course, so did I—but I didn't dare; I was plumb scared! I could hear him and I could feel him. When you're out like that you develop a sixth sense to where you know something is there, but you can't see it or pick it out. I knew he was there watching and waiting in the dense thicket of trees. The stock knew it too. They stood with their ears prickled forward, constantly on the lookout. I kept all the stock tied because I didn't want to take the chance of the bear scaring one of them into the trees.

When we moved on the next day, His Majesty came back out of the trees and started lumbering along behind us again. I named the grizzly His Majesty because he was the biggest bear I'd ever seen and I knew that he was King of this country for sure! Evidently we were crossing his territory and he intended to keep very close tabs on our actions. His method of operation reminded me of another bear that some trappers had told me about. They had called him a "real silver tip" but I knew there is no separate species of silver tip grizzlies. They're simply a bear in one of his seasonal color phases, when his fur is prime and the silver guard hair is predominant. The trappers said this dude followed them faithfully for four days, then disappeared without a sign.

I was praying my grizzly would soon do the same. I'd seen

184

his twelve-inch tracks with the long, sharp claw marks and had no doubt that he could do us mortal damage if he decided to. I also knew he could smell the dried pike I had packed in my saddlebags for groceries. My only hope was that *we* wouldn't turn into groceries for *him*!

Sleep was next to impossible. I was so tired that I didn't think I could stay awake that night. But with being able to "feel" His Majesty out in the timber—and knowing that he was there from the actions of the stock—there was no way that I could shut an eye in sleep.

I Go
Where Angels
Fear to Tread

Our unwelcome guest tagged along for the better part of the next day, then he suddenly disappeared. I knew he wasn't hovering nearby in the trees, because the stock were relaxed and back to normal. I counted my lucky stars that he either got bored, found another source of food, or decided we were far enough from his private haunt!

Just before hitting Teslin Lake, which is a big lake a half-mile across and fifty miles long, I made camp on the northwest shore. I knew we'd be crossing the Teslin River, which feeds into the lake, early the next day. Wasn't too concerned though. Along the cutline I'd passed a survey crew that was supplied by helicopter. The pilot had taken me up and flown me ahead along my route, so I'd seen the river from the air. It didn't look too bad, even though it was about an eighth of a mile across.

From the river bank it was a different story! The opposite side looked very far away. And the current was swifter than what we'd been in before. There really wasn't a lot of choice though. We had to get across the river . . . and the mesh bridge that spanned it was too scary for the horses. Since no feasible detour presented itself, I went ahead and pushed the stock into the river. The water was freezing! It ran right out of a glacier. Not being much of a swimmer, I got off my horse and took ahold of his tail and let him pull me across. The other animals were on a lead rope tied head to tail.

I looked over my shoulder to see how they were doing and realized that we were in trouble. Big trouble! The pack boxes and panniers were filling with water and pulling down Mula and Trashy! So I grabbed my hunting knife and cut the lead shank on my saddle horse to let him go on, then cut the rope on the other horses so they could reach shore. I knew with just saddles on them, they could make it alright.

Then I swam back to Mula. When I got alongside of her I cut the slash ropes and let go of the pack boxes. She gave a ferocious kick and took off okay. Trashy was a different story, however. She was floundering around real bad. The pack boxes had filled up with water and the bedrolls were saturated and dragging her down. Her nose kept going under and she damn near drowned me trying to keep her head up. I steeled myself and managed to cut off Trashy's pack boxes. But she was too exhausted to go, so I also cut the latigos on the saddle and let it float free. As soon as everything was off her, she got a new burst of energy and started fighting again and trying to make it to shore.

Meantime, *I* was in trouble! The freezing water was starting to bind up my muscles, giving me cramps. And I was tired, tired, tired. Every stroke was an effort. I wasn't thinking of Fairbanks, I was just thinking of getting to the other side!! I was barely conscious of what was happening. There was no energy left in me to swim to shore. I could barely dogpaddle and keep my head up. I was scared to death. "Is this the way it feels to drown?" I wondered. I was completely out of gas. I was gone.

Then some inner guide told me to grab ahold of Trashy's tail. If she could get across, I could too. The swift current caught us. I had no feeling. The water was so cold it had numbed me completely. My last thought was "If you make it baby, I'll be there too . . ."

I have no recollection of exactly what happened next. I vaguely remember hitting shore, letting lose of Trashy's tail and passing out. When I awoke I was almost a mile downriver from where we had started to cross. I turned my aching head enough to see the animals strung out maybe half a mile along the river bank. But I was too exhausted to do anything. I flopped back down on the sandy riverbank and slept. It was like the sleep of the dead. I think right then I'd have slept through an earthquake and a tornado all rolled into one!

When I awoke the next time it was late afternoon. I felt human again and very grateful to be alive! Now it was time for clean up. And to see what—if anything—I had left to complete the trip with. It seemed all the stock had survived; they were grazing as if nothing had happened.

I spent the rest of that day and all the next day on my horse, going down the river bank picking up stuff. Fortunately, the current had pushed it all to my side of the river. I picked up my sleeping bag, oats, saddles . . . Of course, everything was soaked! All the films and tapes I had were ruined. I lost my Seiko watch that I'd brought back from Nam—and the fishing gear was nowhere to be found. But all in all I was lucky. I had the gear necessary to continue the trip. I even recovered my hat. What a surprise that the felt hadn't absorbed enough water to sink it. Somebody had certainly been looking out for me!

Whitehorse
on the
Fourth of July

After my ordeal at the Teslin River, I went back to the Alcan Highway. It was a routine ride that day. Lots of people stopped me to chat as they had heard a recent radio interview or knew

Old trapper's cabin on the Alcan Highway.

about the trip from TV and newspaper coverage. I camped about 10 miles outside of Whitehorse and turned in early in spite of the bright evening. When I awoke the next morning, there was four inches of snow on top of my bedroll! That amazed me because it had been up to 80 degrees the day before. Fortunately, the warmth melted the snow quickly.

I hit Whitehorse on the Fourth of July. Trixy and her folks were waiting for me. That gave me a real lift. It was so good to see her again. She was just a city girl who liked horses—and me it seemed.

Whitehorse is an interesting town. They still use old ferry boats with paddle wheels. They transfer people and supplies all around Atland Lake. Since I was now within a couple of days of being back on schedule, things weren't so tight and I decided to spend two or three days there.

When it came out in their local paper that I was a horseshoer, I was swamped! Horseshoers are a rarity in that part of the country. One usually came around about once a year and did all the horses in the area. He hand't been seen for quite some time, so my services were in great demand. I charged $10 a head with them supplying the shoes. Earned enough money to get some shoes for my own stock, replenish my canned goods and still have some left over for gambling.

They had an active Elks Lodge. The brothers put me up in a nice hotel and took me fishing at Atland Lake. Three of the Elks said they had a hot country and western band playing at the hotel where I was staying, so we all went down to get in a little dancing. I had an Elk diamond pin that was given to me at Alamosa on my hat. Naturally, I checked my hat like everybody else and went on in to dance.

When I got ready to leave, somebody had swiped my hat pin! I about turned that cloak room upside down, I was so furious! But nobody had seen anything, nobody knew anything and I was out a diamond hat pin. It really made me burn.

The next day I went about 15 miles out and made camp. I was still furious about losing my pin and the more I thought about it, the madder I got. Decided to go back that night and really scour that coat room. My search the second night didn't fare any better. I cleaned the place out . . . looked from the floor to the rafters, but no pin. Whoever stole it was long gone with my treasure.

To sooth my frustration, I went on over to the Elks Club and got in a poker game. It was just penny ante stuff when I started. But when I stopped, I was over $200 richer! At least it eased things some to know when I put my head down on my sleeping bag, I had lots of bucks in my pocket.

I was riding along the next day, kinda bored and anxious for something to happen when I spotted some ducks paddling on a pond. Put buckshot in my shotgun, dismounted and crawled on my belly to get close enough to get a couple for a meal. I inched my way over this little bank and was almost within range when they took off. I was laying on my belly in an awkward position, but I slipped up my shotgun and fired. The gun was just a few inches from my collarbone. When the shot rang out, my shoulder also exploded in pain. The impact was terrible. I didn't see where the duck I hit landed. All I saw was stars. I was busy rolling around and cussing and hollering at myself for being so dumb not to brace the gun. No damn duck dinner was worth the agony that shoulder gave me!

I soon discovered a much easier way to bag a fowl dinner. Passing through a marshy area, I came upon a flock of ptarmigan, which are a kind of grouse with feathered legs. They are really dumb birds. Instead of flying away at the threat of danger, they squat down right where they are! This, of course, makes them literally a sitting duck (pardon me, a sitting ptarmigan). Not one to miss such an opportunity, I undid my lariat and simply lassoed a couple of them around the neck. The rope efficiently snapped off their heads—and I dined on ptarmigan.

I now had 24 hours of daylight and was riding eight hours on and eight hours off. The weather was weird. One minute it would be 70 or 80 degrees and sunny—and the next minute it would be pouring rain and I'd be grabbing for my slicker. The bugs were unbelievable. As soon as the rain quit it was hot and humid and the horse flies and mosquitoes would swarm. I mudded up the horses a lot, but every time it rained the mud washed off. Had the stock on a heavy grain ration now as the native grass wasn't very good. They were kinda down at this point, being near the end of the trip and all.

When I took an eight hour break, I wouldn't sleep; did that in the saddle. Instead I'd eat or repair tack or go fishing. I had to go inland from the highway to find a stream or lake that wasn't polluted and the fish all gone. But when you got to the right place, the fishing was really good . . . northern pike, brookies, lake trout that would go eight to 14 pounds. The meat was pink and solid and great eating. I also found a nice waterfall nestled among matchstick-like pine trees. It cascaded some 20 feet and was a natural—if somewhat chilly—shower. It felt good to wash off the grime.

I was looking forward to getting into Haines Junction because the people at the Whitehorse Elks Lodge had told an old fella there I was coming. Upon arrival, he had a fat steak waiting to cook, compliments of the Elks. It was good to have some company too.

"Say, Tom, I got a deal set up for you," he told me.

"What sorta deal?"

"Fella by the name of Mike Johnson drives for DC Truck Lines. He's got a run between Whitehorse and Fairbanks. I talked with him yesterday and he'll stop and check with you every day to see if there's anything you need."

"Great! That'll be handier than a pocket on your shirt. That way I can lighten the stock's load and only pack enough rations for two days. We can set up a deal where he can stop along side the road and put out a marker, then set the stuff I need back in the trees?"

"Sure thing. Then you can pick it up when you reach that point. I'll make all the arrangements," my new friend volunteered. The rest of the evening we swapped stories about trapping and women and the Yukon territory. In a way it was good to have somebody to talk to again. But I also knew my days of riding in solitude were numbered. Soon the trip would be over and I'd be headed back to civilization. That is unless something happened . . .

Part Three

Side-by-Side Semis

When I got to the Yukon/Alaska border, I ran into a real hornets nest. I needed papers. I needed brand inspections for the stock. I needed proof of a Coggins test. I had none of these. Most of my papers had been lost in the river escapade. The few I had left were so smeared from all the water they were almost illegible.

It took a day and a half to convince the damn border guard, who was as sour as an unripe plum, that we should be allowed into Alaska. I used the papers for the yellow saddle horse for the buckskin because the guard didin't know the difference between a buckskin and a palomino. Since I now had another bay horse, the old bay's papers worked for him—and they finally let us pass.

As I was crossing into Alaska, my old heart started singing. I was almost there. And in record time: less than six months along the backbone of the whole North American continent!

I was now on a paved road again. That was a big relief. Traveling on horseback you get dirty enough without having dust stirred up in your face constantly by passing vehicles. It wasn't a paved road like in the states, this one was narrow and built up from tundra and rocks. But it sure beat dirt! Another nice stroke of fortune was that Trixy and her family met me again for a short visit. They'd been on a side trip, but were kinda keeping tabs on me to see if I needed any help on this final leg of the journey.

Just before reaching Tetlin Junction the pack string and I were traveling along and rounded a bend in the road . . . only to see two semis coming straight at us drag racing down the highway! These two rigs were barreling along about 70 miles per hour and they were side-by-side! The road was only big enough for *one* truck—and certainly left no room for us! I had no choice but to bail off the bank and take the stock down with me. There wasn't time for a careful descent. We just stumbled and tramped over the big rocks that had built up the road. The horses lurched and blundered down the best they could. The sure-footed mules were in a little better shape.

When we got to the bottom and I started checking the stock, I realized the bay was hurt. He was hobbling along the bottom of the muskeg. His leg wasn't as bad as a compound fracture, but it was sure as hell broke. He was lazy and soft, this one the old horse trader had palmed off, but I wouldn't have wished this on him. There was only one thing to do. I led him off a ways, took my 12-gauge with slugs in it and pulled the trigger. He never felt a thing. It kind of put me in the dumps. I'd drug him a long ways and he was sorta worthless, but it was a sick way for a horse to have to go. And the damn truckers never even slowed down!

At the next pay phone, I called the federal vet to tell what had happened to the bay and where to find him, then headed on up the highway. Pretty soon I spotted a mink somebody had recently run over. Probably one of those damn truckers. Anyway, at camp that night I pelted it out, turning it wrong side out like you're supposed to. Even though I salted it good, the dang flies got to it. That mink had so much oil on the fur that the flies had a feast and the hair started slipping on it. I had to throw it away in the end.

197

The weather was still fluky. You'd be riding in the rain one minute and then it was like somebody turned off a faucet. It was like it'd be raining on your side of the street—but if you crossed over to the other side it would be dry and dusty. Never did see anything like that Alcan Highway!

At Tetlin Junction I met a guy who wanted to buy all my stock when the trip was over. We dickered about a day and a half . . . while he hauled me into the back country and we did some mighty good fishing. We saw a lot of wild herds of buffalo.

Buck taking a well deserved rest.

Buffalo and moose are a major problem for the farmers in that region. No fence will hold them out. Barbed wire to a bull moose is like a five-pound bar bell to a weight lifter. They don't bother to jump over it, they just walk plumb through the four or five strands! Just keep right on walking until it pops and goes down. They're a big threat to the farmer's grain and hay because they can ruin a crop in no time. It's a real quandry, because the game wardens tell the farmers they're not supposed to shoot the dang things!

I had trouble getting out of Tetlin Junction. Everybody was congratulating me and telling me that I had it made. A lot of tourists who had seen me on the Alcan as they were going up, now met me coming back. They were full of praise and good wishes. They'd stop, offer me a drink, or invite me into their campers or trailers for a meal and a visit. Some folks even called ahead and made contact with a saddle club in Fairbanks to ride out and escort me in. Told me to see a guy at the Golden War Bonnet western wear store too. I was only about 150 miles from my goal now. I nearly had it whipped! Those last few miles seemed an unneeded effort. But my goal had always been Fairbanks, so I was determined to push on.

Leaving Tetlin Junction, I started traveling the Alaskan pipeline. There wasn't supposed to be anybody on the pipeline except employees, of course. But I couldn't have made five miles a day on the Alcan with the tourists hounding me constantly. And I didn't want to seem unsociable or ungrateful. This clear cut strip through the forest was a perfect route. It was like the fire lanes on the Yukon border.

I wasn't carrying any canned goods now. Wanted to make it as easy on the stock as possible. If I could fish or get ptarmigan, I ate. If I couldn't, I didn't. All I was packing was horsefeed. I learned to like "cowboy oatmeal." You take horse oats, wash them, bring them to a boil, dump some honey on them and eat!

On July 22nd at Big Delta I made a call home to Colorado and learned some real disappointing news. Before I left we had set up with a P.R. man to come out from California to handle my actual arrival in Fairbanks. I learned the guy was deathly ill and absolutely no publicity had been planned. John Wayne was supposed to meet me outside Fairbanks and ride into town with me and everything. About now it looked like the only thing that was going to ride into Fairbanks with me were the damn bugs! It was all I could do to stick by my motto of Be Tough or Be Gone.

Trixy and her folks were in Big Delta to meet me, so that took some of the edge off my frustration. They volunteered to go in and try to set up some media coverage. They drove into

Fairbanks and made a media whirlwind tour of the radio and TV stations and the newspaper. But unbeknownst to any of us, the 23rd and 24th of July was "Golden Days" in Fairbanks. It is one of the largest summer festivals in Alaska and relives the gold era with festivities, parades and a vast lineup of activities. Everything was already geared up and set. There was no room for a last-minute outsider. My publicity was scooped. Here I was about to break three world records, and it looked like everything was going sour . . .

Fairbanks, Alaska
—Here I Come!

As it actually turned out, "Fairbanks, Alaska, here *we* come" is more true. Luke picked this moment to show up again and grasp a share of the glory. He came ambling up just before the Fairbanks Saddle Club met me on the outskirts of town. They escorted us in.

When I rode into Fairbanks, Alaska on July 23, 1976, I felt like a king! Whether I proved anything to anybody else or not, I proved a bunch to *me*! I did what I set out to do. And even if I didn't have a highfalutin welcome, *I* knew what I had accomplished. I'd proven a person can do anything they set out to do . . . regardless of their background or their know-how. My know-how was to ride a horse. Period. And not even do that hour after hour, day after day, week after week, month after month. It's one thing to be headed for your destination that night. Or to go chase cows or maybe pack in with an outfitter for a week or two. But to string out a pack train and start out down the road, that's a whole different thing.

I'd gotten word to come by the Golden War Bonnet as soon as I got into town, so that's where we headed. When the owner heard I was waiting outside, he came out sporting a broad grin and said, "Welcome! I been waitin' to outfit you. Come on in. Bring your horse too."

201

They propped the doors open wide and the horse and I walked in. Flashbulbs popped like champagne corks as a resourceful reporter took pictures. There I was standing in the stirrups looking down at some mighty surprised sales girls!

Shopping for new duds at the Golden War Bonnet
in Fairbanks, Alaska.

They had their dresses, shirts and pants hanging on portable racks. Well, we dern near wrecked that store! Got in there and went to turn Buck around and he bumped one of the racks and knocked it over. That started a kind of chain reaction, which in turn excited the horse and he went to jumping around and created more havoc.

I was almost too embarrassed to accept the suit of party clothes they pressed on me. Almost, but not quite. I was really ratty looking at the end. I'd thrown everything away except one set of clothes, to cull weight. I had been laundering the clothes on my back when I'd take a bath in a river or lake. I'd use a bar of soap on my shirt and pants, then take them off, rinse them, wash my body, then don the clothes again. At the finish, I looked more like a ragged beggar than a conquering cowboy! But a shower, beard trim and haircut—and the new duds— changed all that.

Next I looked up the guy I'd met back in Tetlin Junction and sold all the stock. I arranged with him to have the use of my saddle horse while I was still in Alaska, so that gave me a way to get around. From the sale, I got enough money to live it up for three or four days. Rented me a room at the Travelers Inn of Alaska for $88.20 a night. Quite a price for a plain-Jane room with no air conditioning, no pool, no special stuff.

Trixy had her Dad's Toyota part of the time—and I had a new suit of clothes—so we lived it up. I had just the one suit, of course. I'd go out all day and evening, return to the hotel, call room service to have it cleaned while I slept, then get dressed in it again the next morning.

The day after I arrived was the big parade. I was invited to ride in it, but not in the fitting spot of Grand Marshall. I thought I should have been leading the parade, not back in fifth or sixth position, so every so often I rode on up to the front. They would get on my case about being out in front. So I'd circle around again, stay in back awhile, then go over the sidewalk and wend my way up to the front again. Meantime, Trixy was walking along with the parade carrying a paper bag. She kept me supplied with "cokes." With each swig I felt more like celebrating!

That evening I was standing at the back door of the Elks Lodge having a toddy for the body when a guy said, "If you bring your animal in, we'd like to take some pictures of you. Like to have one blown up to put on the wall. Besides, I'll buy you a drink if you can get him in."

So in we went, right up along side the bar. Of course, he picked just that time to crap on the floor—and he knocked over a few tables on the way. That was nothing, however, compared to the runners he put in the carpet! I had one drink and figured I'd best make a fast exit. When I started to leave I led Buck across the hardwood dance floor so as not to mess up the carpet any more. Bad choice! The borium on the horseshoes caused him to slip. His fast-moving feet whisked the varnish and wax right off that dance floor in big fat curls.

When I wasn't riding around with Trixy, I'd use Buck for my transportation. Tied to parking meters, he caused quite a sensation in downtown Fairbanks. The police told me, "Cowboy, you can't do that. This isn't the old West. Fairbanks is civilized now. We have taxi service, call a cab." I listened and nodded.

Everyplace I went I drew a crowd. People bought me meals and drinks and caused quite a stir. At the end of the third day the city cops came around and declared they simply "couldn't have a mess on the sidewalks and besides somebody could get kicked and hurt."

My reply was, "Yep. They told me in El Paso I couldn't do this either."

The following morning there was a police car at my hotel bright and early to pick me up and escort me to the airport. I loaded it with all my gear. I checked two riding saddles, two pack saddles, a rifle, pack boxes, panniers, everything . . . like you'd check one suitcase, with no extra charge. Obviously, the airlines were more supportive than the cops. The police were helpful in one way. They were so glad to see me leave they specially packed my rifle for me.

The only things I carried on the plane home to Alamosa, Colorado were my saddlebags and camera. I'd done all the heavy traveling I needed for a long, long time! My journey had turned into an obsession which had to be done. And so it was.

Epilogue

Be Tough or Be Gone is the story of a cowboy with a dream. It's also the story of struggle and growth.

This trip taught me a lot about people. You hear about how unfriendly people are; that everybody in the 20th century is looking after themselves and won't help anybody out. I went 4,500 miles and was only turned down once. It says a lot to me that people are there to help you if you don't try to screw them over. You get what you expect.

I also learned a lot about America and Canada. Things you can't usually find in books or pictures or maps. Now I know how the backbone of the North American continent lays and how it changes. I've felt it and tasted it and smelled it and lived it. You go from scarcely a dessert rat to an abundance of game, from parched dryness to water flowing everywhere, from muskeg to timber so thick a man can't walk through it, from flat land to majestic mountains. I've seen America covered with a light dusting of snow like powdered sugar atop pancakes... and Canada blanketed in white 20 feet deep.

Sure enough, I made it back home in time to ride in the bronc competition at the Ski-Hi-Stampede. And in the weeks to follow to be invited to ride in state fair parades in Colorado, New Mexico, Texas and California. I was voted "Elk of the Month" by the Alamosa Lodge in July of 1976. And I set world records for taking a pack string 4,500 miles in less than six months and crossing three boundaries.

But the most important aspect of this trip is what I learned about myself. When I started out, I didn't think a whole lot of myself. Now that's all changed. I have self-confidence. I know I can go and do and become a success at anything I set out to do. Before I did a lot of things, but I was never really good at any of them. Now I tell the kids in the schools, "You can do anything you want to do if you want to do it bad enough. There is absolutely no such thing as can't." Since the trip, I've come to agree with a wise person who once said, "The only thing that's impossible is what's not tried. The difficult we do right away; the impossible takes a little longer."

Tom Davis has lived with danger most of his life. In his youth, he traveled the rodeo circuit, gathered wild horses, broke and trained roping and cutting horses, worked as a blacksmith and did a stint as a combat helicopter pilot in the Army. More recently, he has trained race horses, owned a bar and supper club and managed a 2,000 acre ranch.

Though born in Albuquerque, New Mexico, Davis has lived in Arizona, Idaho, and Montana. He and his wife and two daughters now make their home in La Jara, Colorado, where he is active in the Elk's, American Legion, Disabled American Veterans, and the Chamber of Commerce.